PARENTS SHAPE SCHOOL SUCCESS

PARENTS SHAPE SCHOOL SUCCESS

A Guide for Parents of Elementary Students

AnnMae Johnson

1997
Galde Press
PO Box 460, Lakeville, Minnesota 55044–0460, U.S.A.

First Edition
First Printing, 1997

Cover by Christopher Wells
Alphabet blocks by George Ostroushko
Design by Susan Van Zant

Library of Congress Cataloging-in-Publication Data

Johnson, AnnMae, 1935–
    Parents shape school success : a guide for parents of elementary
students / AnnMae Johnson. — 1st ed.
        p.   cm.
    ISBN 1–880090–45–7 (pbk.)
    1. Education, Elementary—Parent participation—United States—
Handbooks, manuals, etc.   2. Home and school—United States—
Handbooks, manuals, etc.   I. Title.
LB1048.5.J63   1997
371.19'2—dc21   97–37203
                                                                            CIP

Galde Press, Inc.
PO Box 460
Lakeville, Minnesota 55044

CONTENTS

"Parents are the first and most important of their children's educators."

—Universal Declaration of Human Rights of the United Nations Charter

"The effect that even the best school has on the total education of a child is vastly over-rated and, in comparison with the home...relatively small."

—Neil Postman and Charles Wiengartner, *The School Book*

"Parents should be their children's first teachers."

—President Clinton

PREFACE

ARE your children getting the kind of education that will best prepare them to lead productive and satisfying lives as adults, and successfully meet the challenges of the future? Did you recently move your children to a different school only to find that you are still worried about the quality of education they are receiving? If you are concerned about whether your children are learning all they should know, then this book will help you.

I set forth a new way of looking at education. I offer to put you, the parent, in control of your children's learning so that you can know that they are acquiring a high-quality education. I present plans for you to follow that enable you to work closely with schools in better integrating school and home learning. Further, I urge you to use and support the many resources to be found in your own community that can enrich this learning.

This book has evolved from experiences of over thirty years of teaching all ages of elementary students and educating three children of my own. My convictions have grown from a wide range of personal teaching opportunities, including helping to

■ ■

start an alternative public school. The conclusions are the result of a continual search for ways to best assist parents in helping their children.

My insights were influenced by observing and volunteer teaching in many British schools while studying in Cambridge, England, and by visiting Japanese and Chinese schools. They are the product of personally sharing the deep concerns of parents who are frustrated with their children's school experiences and do not know how to evaluate their achievements.

In this book, I first describe why we need a different approach to education today. As you, the parent, assume the leading role in securing quality education for your children, you need to know about changes in our society that call on you to be diligently involved in the process. You must no longer leave your youngsters' education to the uncertainties of our changing times. You shape your children's school success, so learn how to do it well!

To assist you, I next present a plan of learning outcomes for you to use with your elementary-grade children. It is a guide for monitoring what they have learned and directing what they yet need to study. It can inform you of high-priority areas of study, so that you can fill in those not being covered by school and community activities.

The plan is purposely open-ended so that each family and child can freely choose their own learning path, be as creative as they like, and set their own pace. It leads students to make the appropriate study choices at school as well as at home that enable them to reach the ambitious outcomes they set for themselves. It empowers parents, not to be adversaries of the schools, but to be more effective partners with them.

The program is simple so a working parent can easily manage it. It is meant to be understandable and appropriate for parents of a variety of cultures and education levels. You can expand it at any point to increase the challenge to more able and creative children.

After the education plan, I address the important issue of educational responsibility from the parent, student, school, and community perspectives. As important as homes and schools are in the educational process, parents must look beyond them to gain and support what the whole community offers.

In the final part of the book, I discuss what you need to know about public schools and teachers. I realize that many parents find it difficult to understand the internal dynamics of schools. Aware of this, you will be more effective in relating to teachers and administrators as you shape your children's school success.

CHAPTER 1

A DIFFERENT EDUCATION
FOR A CHANGING WORLD

NEWS now travels around the world in seconds! With fingertip movements we scan a multitude of choices on our television sets to get that news or have other experiences instantly brought to us from faraway places.

We vacation in different countries as if they were places close at hand and spend our leisure time talking with people in other parts of the world via home computers. We pace our shopping malls to buy the latest novel items that are made in many different countries, or the new models that rapidly replace old ones.

The technological advances that make these lifestyle opportunities possible have radically changed the world of work. New jobs are continually being created while others disappear. Many of these now involve bringing daily resources to us that are produced by workers in other countries, or selling our products and services to other parts of the world.

New positions in most careers require workers to learn things quickly, gain multiple skills, and communicate through many different channels. People are increasingly working with their minds rather than their hands, as quicker and more accurate high-tech instruments eliminate routine labor. Most tasks today require as a minimum the ability to organize and interpret information that one gains from and processes on computers.

The jobs that tomorrow's school graduates find will be even less permanent and require portable skills that they can carry from one position to another. Indeed, they will find it necessary to create new jobs in new companies. To succeed in the workplace graduates must be good self-managers as well as team participants. Those who advance the farthest will be the ones who are skilled at flexibly adapting as they move from one project or job to another. This will happen because they also enjoy learning and working with new and challenging ideas.

Just how do we prepare children for the world of work that they will face? Foremost, we must help them to find an ever-increasing pleasure in learning that will motivate them to continually seek knowledge. Then they will not view learning merely as a chore to be only done at school while they are young. From their earliest experiences, children should be led to anticipate the enjoyment found in learning. Then when they grow up they won't want to quit learning after they get that high school diploma. Rather, they will look forward to the intellectual adventures to be found in all realms of life!

Along with this, students need to learn to recognize and quickly master new sources and techniques of learning. The World Wide Web alone provides uncounted information sources, and there is much more potential in the interactive global electronic networks that will be linked by fiber optic cables. Students need to learn to access these sources independently and decide how to apply this treasure of information to their working and leisure lives.

If high quality learning is to become an enjoyable and continuous activity for children, who is responsible to make sure it happens? **This much broader perception of learning required to keep up with the changes in our world and the**

way we work puts you as parent in the best position to guide your children's learning. You are the most constant force in their lives as you supervise their days and shape their choices. They see you as their role model. Ultimately, this makes you accountable.

Just what does this task demand of you, the parent? First, you must **be an excited learner** yourself. Together with your children you can ask questions, wrestle with hard issues, and enthusiastically seek out new viewpoints. You can do research, predict, survey, experiment, and draw conclusions from those experiences.

As a family look for those interconnections in our world by comparing and contrasting new information with what you have already discovered. You can find such challenges in the daily weather reports, news about world events, and the latest scientific discoveries.

Use your home computer, local library, book stores, museums, and other community facilities to **access new information**. Keep written records in notebooks.

Once you have found sufficient information on a subject—whether dogs, earthquakes, or crime, interpret it and share it with others in writing, conversations, and picture form. When you gain the basic information, this may stimulate you and your children to dig deeper into the subject. If, for example, you choose to learn more about dogs, you could see a veterinarian or dog trainer.

Together with your children find ways to **steer and accelerate learning**. The learning plan in the following chapter is a logical starting point. The enthusiasm you draw from having an organized program that sets the direction and shows progress will increase your rate of learning.

Once children know what they want to explore, they usually want to devote more time and energy to their quests. Build on those ideas that your children find especially interesting.

Together, you will find yourselves planning your hours and days around intriguing learning adventures. You may, for instance, pursue topics like famous scientists or musicians for a while and then change to architecture or endangered animals.

As you **let your children take the lead** in their academic discoveries, you will need to **bring them to the places** that broaden their knowledge and provide opportunities to share their new insights with others. Vacations in national and state parks help you to be more aware of geology and biology. To visit a large airport will impress you with how many people and skills are necessary to operate a complex organization. Tours of factories and local businesses demonstrate the many careers available and what a person must do to succeed in them. A trip away from the city lights to stargaze enables you to grasp the challenges of space exploration.

For all of these experiences, you need to help your children keep pictures and observations in **a scrapbook to remember** what they have learned. It is natural for children to want to share what they have discovered with friends, club groups, and at school when it is organized and displayed in an interesting way.

It is also important that you help your children build a rich fund of **knowledge about past happenings** in our world. The learning plan will help you choose what to study. History in the broadest sense is the collected memories of our society. It helps us to understand both the best and worst of human life, and shows us how past generations have contributed to the world we live in today. Children do well to learn some history by tapping the memories of older people.

Knowing our history gives us a richer background for communicating and making decisions. We need to know about the developments and changes of our many civilizations, the wars that have raged, and the ingenuity that people have shown because it enriches our lives and broadens our thinking capacity.

Along with this, your children need to acquire a **global perspective and concern**. Again, the learning program will guide you in studying our many cultures in order to better understand and work with the different people living on our planet. To enrich this experience, you may choose to host international students, attend cultural events, or develop friendships with people with different ethnic backgrounds from your own. Many public television programs stimulate awareness of diverse cultures.

Also, seek to understand **current happenings and future opportunities,** especially in economics, science, and technology. Profound changes keep altering our world. You can read the newspaper and together discuss the information found in the different articles. Ask librarians for suggested readings on topics that attract your attention. Be aware that keeping up with new development in information technology might open up a whole new career for your children, or create a totally different source of learning. As you talk about global and local economic problems that are in the news, view them as opportunities to grow personally and to help others.

Finally, **develop the appropriate attitudes and values** that will enable your youngsters to work effectively with others in our complex and competitive world. Together accept responsibility for yourselves as citizens and then as group members who work toward shared goals.

As a family, you can be a laboratory for settling disagreements peacefully. Learning to respect others goes beyond tolerating differences to showing care and compassion. You can do things for your neighbors, help at nursing homes, and participate as a family in community organizations. All of this requires growth in being open-minded and flexible, while taking a stand for what is fair and honest.

Keep in mind that this kind of education which is needed for life in the 21st century demands more than we can reasonably count on schools today to do by themselves. Our educational systems do try one reform after another, but they usually disappoint us because the improvements we most want can't be attained without close parental involvement. **We can no longer expect the schools to do it all!**

Public schools now serve a wider range of students including some who require many special services. The curriculum is thus loaded with social learning requirements to meet these needs. Educators need to cover personal health and safety, drug and sexual abuse, family life, aging and death education, career and consumer choices, community service and global awareness, character development and peace education. Such learning experiences are to be multi-cultural, gender-fair, developmentally appropriate, and include the physically challenged. These demands reduce the time that teachers can spend on the increased academic requirements they must also meet.

Because of this, schools are limited in what they can do to educate masses of students in the normal school day, especially when funding is restricted. Often teachers cannot give your children the kind of personal learning attention you prefer.

Unquestionably, it is important for all students to develop a good self-concept as they learn to work cooperatively. It is equally valuable for them to learn respect and responsibility as they plan and carry out community service projects.

Unfortunately, time spent on teaching these social concepts reduces the time available to teach the essentials of math, science, communication skills, social studies, and the arts. Time constraints imposed by many competing expectations can force academic instruction to be watered down or mass delivered and fragmented. Classroom teachers have only so much time and energy, and no magical powers.

Since children are learning all day long and much of what they learn takes place outside of their school time, **you, the parent, are in the best place to guide learning growth**. Actually, you are in a better position than teachers to develop self-esteem, respect for others, faith, and responsibility in all areas of behavior. You can also teach or enrich their understanding of math, reading, science, and other academic areas.

I realize that you lead busy lives, particularly those of you who must work outside the home. Your time as a teacher may be very limited, but with a workable plan, such as the one I set forth in the next chapter, you can use productively even the odd half-hour and mealtime conversations. I know because I myself worked while raising three children. I can truly confirm that parents do shape student success!

Many of you have the advantage today of being well-educated yourselves. Your small families, too, make this task more manageable. It is an undertaking, however, that any parent can do. If you feel inadequate, just learn right along with your children. Continual learning is the essence of good teaching, and it will enrich both your life and your family's. If your teaching time is limited, plan and use well what you do have. Begin with just a few things that will get you moving in the right direction. Always remember that you are in the best place to personalize and expand your children's learning.

To assist you, we now have interactive multimedia technology that can make learning more exciting and effective. It can shorten learning time and increase children's retention. With technology you can choose from an enormous menu, and then study when and where it is convenient. Video disks and interactive learning games are rapidly becoming available in public and school libraries, a service for those who cannot afford to buy them.

Your children's planned education ought not be limited to their few school hours. **You must make your home the primary stimulant to their independent learning, so they can also make the most of their time in the classroom.** In this way you as parent can know for certain that your children are getting the leading edge that a high quality education provides!

CHAPTER 2

INDIVIDUAL LEARNING PLAN

THE plan that follows is an elementary curriculum guide for setting goals and evaluating learning progress. Together, as parent and student, develop your own study program to go with it. Establish weekly, monthly, and annual goals, and chart progress toward them. Decide what to study and how to acquire the needed knowledge and skills.

For some concepts you will choose to develop projects after completing surveys and interviews. For others you may visit places in the community. Almost all learning experiences can be enhanced by checking books out of the library.

Keep neat records of your experiences in inexpensive spiral or loose-leaf notebooks. Review and evaluate these to inspire and direct future progress. After checking with classroom teachers, decide what to study. Students can look in newspapers or magazines when investigating mathematical problems. They can help with grocery shopping and meal preparation to learn to calculate quantities and prices of ingredients.

If you do not understand some concepts, together consult an encyclopedia or ask a librarian or a teacher. Knowing where to find the information is a very important skill to learning independently. Discoveries can be found in many sources—people, books, first-hand observations, and the Internet.

Scrapbooks provide good places to record reading experiences. They can be used to display pictures and descriptions from trips to businesses, museums, parks and zoos. Reports on and reactions to books can be put in them, as well as art projects. Scrapbooks can help children share their experiences with relatives, club groups, and school classes. Someday they can be used to help recall growing-up thoughts and experiences!

Use charts and graphs to visually display information and progress. As you work to build good lifetime health habits, chart growth in physical exercise and fitness, and in eating nutritious foods. Put these records into notebooks for evaluating your long term progress.

Keep in mind that your most important goal is to become independent thinkers who know how to learn and can work with others. Analyzing, describing, and comparing ideas and information are better ways to increase thinking ability than just giving brief answers to the questions in a learning plan.

Have fun learning together! Take pleasure in discovering new information! Enjoy discussing ideas with each other!

■■■■■■■■■■■■■■■■■■■■■■■■■■■■■■■■■

Learning Plan
for

_____

(Name of Student)

At regular intervals, weekly or monthly, show progress using the number markings below. Continue to review and expand your knowledge of these concepts after initial proficiency has been established.

Set your own ambitious rate of learning! Although the skills and understandings that fall into logical order for learning are presented by grade level, you can select your own order of study. Plan to excel in understanding all areas.

1. Exploring/Discovering

2. Developing

3. Proficient

Specific Grade Level Skills

FIRST GRADE SKILLS

Communication Skills

Reading

___ Reads independently for at least ten minutes a day.

___ Chooses appropriate reading material with understandable words and beneficial content.

___ Recognizes many frequently used words.

___ Uses context clues, the sounds letters usually represent, and other strategies to figure out how to pronounce unknown words.

___ Gives sounds for consonant letters in isolation.

___ Gives short vowel sounds in isolation.

___ Blends consonant and vowel sounds to pronounce words.

Writing

___ Writes upper and lower case manuscript letters correctly.

___ Writes neatly.

___ Frequently writes ideas down on paper.

___ Writes sentences.

Speaking

___ Frequently shares personal experiences and stories.

___ Retells stories and rhymes.

___ Discusses familiar stories and topics with others.

Listening

___ Listens attentively to stories and poems being read aloud.

___ Paraphrases what another person has said.

___ Remembers oral directions with one or two steps.

___ Listens to conversations and can summarize what was discussed.

Mathematics

Math concepts should be taught and tested using familiar story problems and real objects whenever appropriate.

___ Recognizes, copies, interprets, extends and creates simple geometric and number patterns.

___ Sorts and classifies real objects, and uses numbers to compare them.

___ Explains how numerals represent groups of real things, and that each symbol is called a digit.

___ Groups objects correctly to show numbers at least to 100, and writes the numeral for each.

___ Reads the words for numbers through 100.

___ Recognizes ordinal numbers at least through 10.

___ Groups and counts numbers by ones, twos, fives, and tens at least to 100.

___ Tells the numbers that come before and after a given number.

___ Counts backwards from 50.

___ Explains place value: where a numeral is placed determines the value it represents.

___ Gives the place value of a given numeral at least to 100.

___ Adds and subtracts with real objects and writes the notation.

___ Adds and subtracts two-digit numbers without trading.

___ Uses symbols for greater than (>), less than (<) and equals (=) to compare numbers.

___ Estimates quantity with reasonable accuracy.

___ Tells the value of American coins.

___ Reads calendars.

___ Tells time by the hour and half hour.

___ Measures length using inches on a ruler.

___ Measures capacity using cups and pints, and weight using ounces and pounds.

___ Names flat and solid geometric shapes: triangle, rectangle, square, circle, prism, pyramid, oval, diamond, cube and sphere.

___ Builds graphs with real objects, pictures, bars, and tally marks, and interprets them.

___ Describes parts of a whole or parts of a group of things using the fractions halves, thirds, and quarters.

___ Finds answers to simple story problems by using objects, drawing pictures, and by writing the notation.

Geography

___ Makes maps of his or her house, classroom, and neighborhood.

___ Describes the four directions on a map.

___ Locates continents and oceans, polar and equatorial regions on a map.

___ Compares globes with a variety of other maps.

___ Locates where he or she lives on a globe and a flat map.

SECOND GRADE SKILLS

Communication

Reading

____ Reads independently for at least fifteen minutes a day.

____ Chooses appropriate reading material with understandable words and beneficial content.

____ Reads both fiction and nonfiction literature.

____ Uses context clues, the sounds letters usually represent, and other strategies to figure out how to pronounce unknown words.

____ Describes the sequence of events in a story which sometimes have signal words like after, next, and then.

____ Identifies compound words and contractions.

____ Discusses what he or she has read and compares stories.

Writing

____ Writes, shares, and saves own stories and poems.

____ Writes in complete sentences.

____ Uses capital letters correctly at beginning of sentences, for proper nouns, months, and days of the week.

____ Uses punctuation marks at the end of sentences.

____ Identifies prefixes and suffixes that are added to base words.

____ Spells many frequently used words accurately.

____ Writes neatly and shapes letters correctly in manuscript.

____ Writes some letters and words in cursive.

Speaking

___ Frequently shares what he or she has read or experienced.

___ Summarizes events or the content of what was read.

___ Recites poems.

___ Tells imaginative stories.

Listening

___ Listens attentively to stories and poems being read aloud.

___ Paraphrases what another person has said.

___ Listens to conversations and summarizes what was discussed.

___ Follows oral directions with two to three steps.

Mathematics

Math concepts should be taught and tested using familiar story problems and real objects whenever appropriate.

___ Locates, interprets, and creates number and geometric patterns.

___ Compares groups of objects by recognizing the attributes like different numbers, colors, and shapes.

___ Identifies odd and even numbers.

___ Counts forward and backward at least to 250, stopping and starting again.

___ Recognizes ordinal numbers at least through thirty.

___ Compares numbers at least to 999 using symbols for greater than (>), less than (<), or equal to (=).

___ Compares groups of objects by using words like more, less, most, least, more than, and less than.

___ Explains addition and subtraction by using objects and drawing pictures.

___ Explains family of facts (4 + 5 = 9, 5 + 4 = 9, 9 − 5 = 4, 9 − 4 = 5).

___ Recalls quickly the basic addition and subtraction facts.

___ Adds and subtracts two-digit numbers by regrouping with objects.

___ Tells the place value of each digit in numbers to 9,999, and writes numbers in expanded form (649 = 600 + 40 + 9).

___ Finds the answers to multiplication problems with factors from 0 to 5 using objects.

___ Measures and compares length, width, height, and perimeter.

___ Estimates numbers of objects in a small group with reasonable accuracy.

___ Tells time by the quarter hour and five-minute intervals.

___ Counts groups of coins to 100 cents.

___ Solves real purchasing problems involving the exchange of coins up to one dollar.

___ Makes and interprets picture graphs, tally charts, and bar graphs.

___ Compares plane figures like circles, squares, triangles, and rectangles to solid figures like spheres, cubes, cones, and cylinders.

___ Locates the line of symmetry in symmetrical objects.

___ Uses the fractions halves, thirds, quarters, and eighths to describe parts of a whole or parts of a group of things.

___ Solves story problems by adding and subtracting real objects, drawing pictures, and writing the notation.

___ Adds and subtracts using a number line.

___ Checks subtraction with addition and vice versa.

___ Sets up and solves problems on calculators.

___ Lists ways her or his family uses math in their daily lives.

Geography

___ Makes maps of her or his school and neighborhood.

___ Locates nearby places using a map.

___ Describes locations on a map using cardinal directions.

___ Compares continents with oceans, polar with equatorial regions.

___ Locates where on a globe and flat map he or she lives.

___ Locates and names a few of the big countries and cities on our planet.

___ Compares the geographic features of North America with those of South America.

THIRD GRADE SKILLS

Communications

Reading

___ Reads independently for at least twenty minutes a day.

___ Chooses appropriate reading material with understandable words and beneficial content.

___ Categorizes books by reference, fiction, and nonfiction.

___ Reads different kinds of literature including fiction and nonfiction: biography, fantasy, poetry, science, and history.

___ Uses context clues, the sounds letters usually represent, and other strategies to figure out how to pronounce unknown words.

___ Uses a dictionary to learn the meaning of unknown words.

___ Discusses what he or she has read and compares the ideas with other material that has been read.

___ Identifies, in fiction works, the story setting, main characters, and plot.

___ Draws conclusions and predicts outcomes for a story.

___ Distinguishes between reality and fantasy when reading.

___ Recognizes similes and other figurative language.

___ Uses the title page, table of contents, glossary, and index to learn information about a book.

PARENTS SHAPE SCHOOL SUCCESS

Writing

___ Writes, shares, and saves own stories and poems.

___ Writes poetry with repetition, alliteration, and simile.

___ Writes in complete sentences.

___ Identifies incomplete and run-on sentences.

___ Tries different arrangements of words and phrases in a sentence when expressing ideas in writing.

___ Uses capital letters correctly.

___ Uses punctuation marks at the end of sentences and for conversations.

___ Identifies nouns, pronouns, adjectives, verbs, prefixes, suffixes, antonyms, synonyms, and abbreviations.

___ Spells frequently used words correctly.

___ Recognizes when the suffixes of "ed, ing, y, s, and es" have been added to base words, and how the spelling is sometimes changed.

___ Writes neatly and shapes letters correctly in both manuscript and cursive writing.

Speaking

___ Speaks clearly and distinctly, enunciating words.

___ Shares personal experiences.

___ Discusses familiar stories and topics with others, asking questions and comparing ideas.

Listening

___ Listens attentively to different forms of literature being read aloud and summarizes what was read.

___ Paraphrases what another person has said.

___ Summarizes news stories.

___ Remembers oral directions.

___ Listens attentively to conversations, providing eye contact with the speaker.

Mathematics

___ Locates, interprets, and creates complex number and geometric patterns.

___ Compares groups of objects by recognizing various attributes like different numbers, colors, sizes, shapes, and positions.

___ Explains strategies that help solve math problems: use real objects and act it out, draw a picture, break it into easier steps or parts, guess and then check, look for patterns, work backwards, or make lists.

___ Creates story problems for self and others to solve.

___ Estimates answers to problems.

___ Finds the average of several numbers.

___ Adds and subtracts large numbers with regrouping.

___ Gives the place value of a given numeral.

___ Writes large numbers from dictation through 999,999.

___ Quickly recalls the multiplication facts to 9 x 9 and the corresponding division facts.

___ Checks multiplication with division and vice versa.

___ Analyzes errors when correcting wrong answers.

■ ■

___ Writes number equations in expanded form: 48 – 23 = (40 + 8) – (20 + 3)].

___ Rounds numbers by tens, hundreds, and thousands.

___ Writes the notation and draws pictures of simple fractions.

___ Compares the sizes of two simple fractions (<, >, =).

___ Uses a number line to explain fractions, addition, subtraction, multiplication, and division.

___ Compares two-dimensional with three-dimensional figures, and names some examples.

___ Labels vertexes, sides, and angles of plane figures and vertexes, edges, and faces of solids.

___ Explains the difference between congruent and symmetrical figures.

___ Constructs line and bar graphs to solve story problems.

___ Compares (<, >, =) inches, feet, yards, miles, centimeters, meters, and kilometers.

___ Measures length, width, and perimeter of an area.

___ Adds and subtracts coins up to one dollar.

___ Tells time by the minute.

___ Recognizes Roman numerals through 20.

___ Compares the amount of time between various days on the calendar, and solves problems involving time.

___ Measures weight of objects by ounces and pounds, grams, and kilograms.

___ Compares liquid measurements of cup, pint, fluid ounce, quart, gallon, and liter.

___ Sets up and solves problems on calculators.

___ Describes ways in which family uses math in daily life.

Geography

___ Makes maps of his or her neighborhood and community.

___ Locates places in her or his state using a map.

___ Describes locations on a map using cardinal directions.

___ Names the continents and oceans, polar and equatorial regions.

___ Explains how the earth rotates around the sun.

___ Locates his or her state on a globe and a variety of maps.

___ Locates major rivers, mountain ranges, and cities on a map.

___ Names some of the largest countries on each continent.

___ Compares the major geographic features of North America and South America with those of Africa.

FOURTH GRADE SKILLS

Communications

Reading

____ Reads independently for at least twenty-five minutes a day.

____ Reads a variety of fiction and nonfiction literature: biographies, novels, short stories, poetry, essays, and magazine articles.

____ Uses a dictionary to learn the meaning of unknown words.

____ Describes how adding prefixes and suffixes to base words sometimes changes the meaning of the word.

____ Divides words into syllables.

____ Discusses what she or he has read and compares it with previous reading.

____ Identifies, in fiction works, an author's purpose and point of view, story setting, main characters, plot, and conflicts.

____ Distinguishes between fact and opinion, main ideas and details, reality and fantasy when reading.

____ Draws conclusions, makes generalizations, and predicts outcomes when reading a story.

____ Recognizes analogies and other figurative language.

____ Uses the title page, table of contents, glossary, and index to locate information about a book.

____ Locates alphabetized information such as that found in encyclopedias and telephone directories.

Writing

___ Writes, shares, and saves own stories and poems.

___ Uses similes and analogies when writing.

___ Tries different arrangements of words and phrases in a sentence when expressing ideas in writing.

___ Writes poetry in different styles, such as free verse with creative endings.

___ Writes sentences with correct capitalization and punctuation.

___ Uses paragraphs when writing stories, journal entries, formal reports, dialogues, and descriptions.

___ Writes letters and addresses envelopes correctly.

___ Writes research reports with bibliography and graphic aids.

___ Uses the writing steps of prewriting, drafting, revising, and proofreading.

___ Identifies nouns, pronouns, adjectives, verbs, adverbs, prepositions, conjunctions, antonyms, synonyms, homophones, and abbreviations.

___ Recognizes and corrects spelling mistakes, sometimes keeping a list of words to learn to spell.

___ Shapes letters correctly and writes neatly in both cursive and manuscript writing.

Speaking

___ Speaks clearly and distinctly, enunciating words

___ Discusses current news topics, asking questions and comparing ideas.

▪▪▪▪▪▪▪▪▪▪▪▪▪▪▪▪▪▪▪▪▪▪▪▪▪▪▪▪▪▪▪▪

___ Summarizes stories and describes events succinctly.

___ Gives oral instructions to others in a group.

Listening

___ Listens attentively to many different forms of literature being read aloud, and displays understanding in follow-up discussions.

___ Remembers oral directions.

___ Listens attentively to conversations and participates by seeking clarification and adding to the sustained discussion of a given topic.

Mathematics

___ Recognizes complex geometric and number patterns.

___ Compares groups of objects using the attributes of different color, size, shape, position, texture, number, and thickness.

___ Communicates an understanding of mathematical concepts (multiplication, division, fractions, decimals) orally and in writing by using objects or drawing pictures.

___ Describes strategies that help solve math problems: use objects, draw pictures, compare it with a simpler problem, guess and check, look for patterns, work backwards, use reasoning, or make charts.

___ Estimates answers when solving problems.

___ Finds the average of several numbers.

___ Adds and subtracts large numbers (thousands, millions, billions).

■ ■

___ Checks subtraction with addition and division with multiplication, and vice versa.

___ Gives the place value of a numeral and can use expanded notation to solve equations (396 = 300 + 90 + 6).

___ Quickly recalls the multiplication facts of numbers through 12 x 12 and the corresponding division facts.

___ Recalls the factors of a given number to 100 (6 x 4, 12 x 2, and 8 x 3 for 24).

___ Explains several ways to multiply and divide.

___ Analyzes errors when correcting wrong answers.

___ Understands the purpose of brackets in a long equation: (6 x 7) + 5 = (7 x 7) – 2.

___ Calculates the number that a letter represents in an equation (8 x n = 32).

___ Correctly uses the terms addend, sum, difference, multiple, factor, product, quotient, divisor, and dividend.

___ Identifies by name numerators, denominators, equivalent fractions, mixed numbers, and improper fractions.

___ Compares (<, >, =) numbers and fractions.

___ Draws pictures for fractions and decimals.

___ Adds and subtracts fractions and mixed numbers.

___ Reduces fractions to lowest terms, and writes equivalent fractions.

___ Adds and subtracts decimals.

___ Uses a number line to explain fractional parts, and addition, subtraction, multiplication, and division.

___ Rounds whole numbers, decimals, and fractions.

___ Locates angles, rays, perpendicular lines, and parallel lines.

___ Identifies similar, congruent, and symmetrical figures.

___ Compares lines, planes, triangles, quadrilaterals, trapezoids, parallelograms, squares, and rectangles and computes the area.

___ Calculates the perimeter and area of a plane figure.

___ Compares two-dimensional solid figures such as pyramids, cylinders, rectangular prisms, and spheres.

___ Identifies the faces, vertexes and edges of cubic structures and calculates the volume.

___ Solves problems using both customary and metric units.

___ Measures weight of objects by ounces, pounds, grams, and kilograms.

___ Compares (>, <, =) liquid measurements of cup, pint, quart, fluid ounce, gallon, and liter.

___ Constructs picture, line, pie and bar graphs to solve math problems.

___ Graphs coordinate numbers.

___ Uses inches, feet, yards, centimeters, and meters to measure and compare length, width, and perimeter of an area or three-dimensional object.

___ Uses addition, subtraction, multiplication, and division to solve story problems involving money.

___ Compares (<, >, =) seconds, minutes, hours, days, months, and years, and adds and subtracts time amounts to solve problems.

___ Compares Celsius and Fahrenheit temperature readings.

___ Recognizes Roman numerals through 100.

___ Sets up and solves problems on calculators.

___ Explains ways he or she will use math in daily living.

Geography

___ Locates places on a map using longitude and latitude lines.

___ Locates the Tropic of Cancer, Tropic of Capricorn, North and South Poles, hemispheres, and prime meridian.

___ Compares the regions of the United States: Pacific Northwest, West, Southwest, Great Plains, Midwest, South, Mid-Atlantic, and New England.

___ Explains the relation of the earth to other planets, including rotation and the effects of the sun on them.

___ Names some of the largest countries on each continent.

___ Makes maps of his or her state and country showing the major geographic features.

___ Compares the most important features of North America and South America with those of Africa and Asia.

FIFTH GRADE SKILLS

Communication

Reading

___ Reads independently for at least thirty minutes a day.

___ Chooses a wide variety of fiction and nonfiction reading materials with beneficial content.

___ Uses a dictionary to learn the meanings of unknown words and how to pronounce them.

___ Recognizes word syllables, accent and stress marks.

___ Shows continual growth in interpretive and critical thinking skills when comparing ideas about what was read.

___ Identifies an author's purpose and point of view.

___ Describes, in fiction works, the relationships and tensions of characters, draws conclusions and makes generalizations.

___ Recognizes similes, metaphors, and analogies.

___ Distinguishes between literal and figurative language.

___ Recognizes and critically appraises exaggeration, persuasion and propaganda in fiction works and advertising.

Writing

___ Writes, shares, and saves stories, essays, and poems.

___ Writes in a variety of forms for many purposes and audiences.

___ Uses correct spelling, capitalization, and punctuation.

___ Writes informative research reports with bibliography and graphic aids.

___ Recognizes the poetry features of stanzas, rhyme and rhythm scheme, meter, and free verse.

___ Identifies subjects and predicates, articles, prepositions, conjunctions, regular and irregular verbs, helping verbs, verb tenses, direct and indirect objects, proper and personal pronouns, nominative, objective, and possessive cases for pronouns, and possessive pronouns.

___ Writes neatly in both cursive and manuscript.

Speaking

___ Enunciates words clearly and correctly.

___ Shares personal experiences and discusses current news topics.

___ Gives short oral presentations on given topics.

___ Debates familiar topics.

___ Varies appropriately the pitch and volume of voice, and the rate of speaking.

___ Converses with appropriate timing and choice of words, sharing the speaking time with another person.

Listening

___ Listens attentively to oral presentations, and makes relevant responses.

___ Summarizes information given in oral presentations.

___ Listens attentively during conversations, participating by seeking clarification and adding to the sustained discussion of a given topic.

Mathematics

___ Explains several ways to quickly calculate large numbers.

___ Explains why remainders in division problems can be written as fractions.

___ Explains why decimals can be written as fractions.

___ Multiplies and divides fractions and decimals.

___ Reduces fractions to lowest terms and writes equivalent fractions.

___ Explains fractions and decimals by drawing pictures and using number lines.

___ Changes decimals and fractions to percentages.

___ Calculates the number that a letter represents in an equation ($6n = 24$).

___ Locates and uses geometric notations to describe angles, rays, perpendicular lines, and parallel lines.

___ Explains the differences between similar, congruent, and symmetrical figures.

___ Measures angles and compares them in triangles, quadrilaterals, trapezoids, parallelograms, squares, and rectangles.

___ Calculates the area of two-dimensional objects, such as triangles and parallelograms, with customary and metric units.

___ Calculates the volume of three-dimensional objects, such as cubes and prisms, with customary and metric units.

___ Explains ratio and scale.

___ Changes metric units to customary, and vice versa.

___ Constructs picture, line, circle and bar graphs to solve math problems.

___ Constructs coordinate number graphs.

___ Compares (<, >, =) inches, feet, yards, miles, centimeters, meters, and kilometers when calculating the length, width, and perimeter of an area or figure.

___ Solves story problems involving the exchange of currency.

___ Compares measurements of time (137 minutes > 2¼ hours) and solves problems involving time.

___ Multiplies and divides time amounts of seconds, minutes, hours, days, months, and years.

___ Recognizes Roman numerals through 1,000.

___ Sets up and solves problems on calculators.

___ Uses all math skills acquired at previous levels, applying them to more challenging problems using more advanced reasoning.

___ Explains why math skills are important in daily living.

Geography

___ Names the hemispheres of the earth.

___ Compares time zones and explains their relationship to the prime meridian.

___ Explains how graphic displays like atlases, charts and graphs can help us to compare geographic data.

___ Locates the world's largest deserts, highest mountains, biggest peninsulas, biggest straits and gulfs, longest channels and rivers, and largest cities on a map.

___ Explains the interrelationship of the urban, suburban, and rural areas.

___ Identifies and compares the provinces of Canada.

___ Makes maps of her or his state and country with a key and scale, showing the various geographic features.

___ Compares the major land and population characteristics of North and South America with those of Africa, Asia, and Europe.

SIXTH GRADE SKILLS

Communication

Reading

____ Reads daily for information and pleasure.

____ Chooses a wide variety of fiction and nonfiction reading material with beneficial content.

____ Discusses what he or she has read, and shows growth in interpretive and critical thinking skills when comparing ideas.

____ Identifies an author's purpose and point of view.

____ Describes story settings, mood, structure, and tensions.

____ Distinguishes between literal and figurative language.

____ Recognizes multiple meanings of words and phrases, and explains inferences and the many possible interpretations.

____ Analyzes and compares the characters in various stories and books.

____ Recognizes and critically appraises exaggeration, persuasion and propaganda as seen in literature, newspapers, magazines, and other forms of advertising.

Writing

____ Writes, shares, and saves stories, essays, reports, and poems.

____ Writes in a variety of forms for many purposes and audiences.

____ Writes lengthy informative research reports with bibliography and graphic aids.

___ Writes both first and third person narratives.

___ Expresses thoughts and emotions in different forms of poetry.

___ Identifies subjects, predicates, articles, prepositions, conjunctions, regular and irregular verbs, helping verbs, verb tenses, direct and indirect objectives, proper and personal pronouns, and possessive pronouns.

___ Recognizes independent and dependent clauses, and simple and complex sentences.

___ Spells and writes accurately and neatly.

Speaking

___ Enunciates words clearly and correctly.

___ Shares personal experiences and discusses current news topics.

___ Gives short oral presentations on given topics.

___ Debates familiar topics from either the affirmative or negative side of the issue.

___ Varies appropriately the pitch and volume of voice, and the rate of speaking.

___ Converses with appropriate timing and choice of words, sharing the speaking time with another person.

Listening

___ Listens attentively to oral presentations, showing genuine interest by making relevant responses.

___ Summarizes succinctly information given in an oral presentation.

___ Listens attentively when talking with another person,

showing genuine interest in what the person is saying by providing eye contact and nonverbal encouragement, and seeking clarification where needed.

<u>Mathematics</u>

___ Creates challenging story problems for others to solve.

___ Estimates answers when solving problems.

___ Computes exponents and square roots of numbers.

___ Explains why division problems can be written as fractions.

___ Calculates simple probability.

___ Recognizes reciprocal numbers.

___ Multiplies and divides decimals, fractions and mixed numbers.

___ Explains why decimals can be written as fractions and vice versa.

___ Rounds whole numbers, mixed numbers and decimals.

___ Changes decimals and fractions to percentages.

___ Solves simple algebraic equations.

___ Calculates data involving positive and negative numbers.

___ Names and writes symbols for points, lines, rays, line segments, angles, parallel lines, and perpendicular lines.

___ Sets up and solves problems that require graphing coordinate numbers.

___ Constructs varying kinds of angles and triangles, and classifies them.

___ Compares polyhedrons: hexagonal, triangular, and rectangular prisms with pentagonal, rectangular, and triangular pyramids.

___ Compares and measures parallelograms, squares, trapezoids, rhombuses, and rectangles.

___ Constructs drawings to scale, specifying the ratio.

___ Calculates volume of solid figures.

___ Measures length, mass, and capacity with customary and metric units.

___ Constructs picture, line, circle and bar graphs to solve math problems and portray information.

___ Calculates and compares time intervals of seconds, minutes, hours, days, months, and years, and solves problems involving them.

___ Sets up and solves problems on calculators.

___ Calculates and compares prices and quantities relationships in purchasing supplies.

___ Calculates percentage discounts and savings when purchasing merchandise.

___ Calculates quantities and prices of supplies needed for food preparation, home improvement projects, and leisure time equipment.

___ Uses all math skills acquired at previous levels, applying them to more challenging problems using more advanced reasoning.

___ Explains why the study of mathematics is important to her or his future.

■ ■

<u>Geography</u>

___ Explains the concept of continent drift and plate tectonics.

___ Compares continental with island settlements.

___ Describes how the geographical features of a region affect the people and the environment.

___ Explains some of the interconnections of people, cultures, climates, and environments around the world.

___ Explains the interrelationships of different human activities in a given geographic area.

___ Compares Mexico with the other countries in Central America and the Caribbean.

___ Makes maps of the different continents with a key and scale, showing the various land features.

___ Names and locates most of the countries on each continent and shares important information about them.

■ ■

Nongraded Concepts and Experiences

LITERATURE

What we read impacts what and how we think! Therefore, read widely and select beneficial literature. Fiction books ought to portray characters with praiseworthy attitudes. Find nonfiction books that are well written and authentic.

Your reading should prepare you with the attitudes and skills to be a contributing member of our society. Choose books that promote commendable character traits like honesty, diligence, patience, tolerance, and creativity and that help you understand the many cultures in our world.

A small sampling of books are listed below to guide you in selecting reading material. To gain more insight into an author or culture, read other books written by the same person or on similar subjects. Ask reference librarians for current lists of recommended books. Keep a list of all your readings in order to evaluate your progress.

African-American and African Stories

Primary

___ Read and discussed *Ragtime Trumpet* by Allan Schroeder.

___ Read and discussed *Boundless Grace* by Mary Hoffman.

___ Read and discussed *John Henry* by Julius Lester.

___ Read and discussed *The Black Snowman* by Phil Mendez.

___ Read and discussed *Working Cotton* by Shirley Anne Williams.

___ Read and discussed *Zora Hurston and the Chinaberry Tree* by William Miller.

___ Read and discussed_____

___ Read and discussed_____

Intermediate

___ Read and discussed *Pink and Say* by Patricia Polacco.

___ Read and discussed *The Well: David's Story* by Mildred P. Taylor.

___ Read and discussed *Stitching Stars: The Story Quilts of Harriet Powers* by Mary Lyons.

___ Read and discussed *Children of Promise* by Charles Sullivan.

___ Read and discussed *Chevrolet Sundays* by Candy Dawson Boyd.

___ Read and discussed *Stealing Home* by Mary Stolz.

___ Read and discussed _____

___ Read and discussed _____

Hispanic-American, Central and South American Stories

Primary

___ Read and discussed *Moon Rope: A Peruvian Folktale* by Lois Ehler.

___ Read and discussed *The Tree that Rains: The Flood Myth of the Huichol Indians of Mexico* by Emery Bernhard.

___ Read and discussed *Caribbean Canvas* by Frane Lessac.

___ Read and discussed *Coconut Kind of Day: Island Poems* by Lynn Joseph.

___ Read and discussed *Amelia's Road* by Linda Jacobs Altman.

___ Read and discussed *Radio Man* by Arthur Dorros.

___ Read and discussed_____

___ Read and discussed_____

Intermediate

___ Read and discussed *Grab Hands and Run* by Frances Temple.

___ Read and discussed *Standing Tall: The Stories of Ten Hispanic Americans* by Argentina Palacios.

___ Read and discussed *The Enchanted Raisin: A Family of Brazil* by Olivia Bennett.

___ Read and discussed *Baseball in April and Other Stories* by Gary Sota.

___ Read and discussed *Voices From the Fields: Children of Migrant Farm Workers Tell Their Stories* by Beth Atkin.

___ Read and discussed *Where Angels Glide at Dawn: New Stories from Latin America* by Lori Carlson and Cynthia Ventura.

___ Read and discussed_____

___ Read and discussed_____

Native American Stories

Primary

___ Read and discussed *The Legend of the Indian Paintbrush* by Tomie DePaola.

___ Read and discussed *This Land Is My Land* by George Littlechild.

___ Read and discussed *Dreamcatcher* by Audrey Osofsky.

___ Read and discussed *Baby Rattlesnake* by Te Ata.

___ Read and discussed *Fox Song* by Joseph Bruchac.

___ Read and discussed *Crow Chief* by Paul Goble.

___ Read and discussed *Arctic Memories* by Mormee Ekooniak.

___ Read and discussed_____

___ Read and discussed_____

Intermediate

___ Read and discussed *The Girl Who Married the Moon: Tales from Native North America* by Joseph Bruchac and Gayle Ross.

___ Read and discussed *Happily May I Walk: American Indians and Alaska Natives Today* by Arlene Hirschielder.

___ Read and discussed *How Rabbit Tricked Otter: And Other Cherokee Trickster Stories* by Gayle Ross.

___ Read and discussed *Pueblo Storyteller* by Diane Hoyt-Goldsmith.

___ Read and discussed *Anna's Athabaskan Summer* by Arnold Greise.

___ Read and discussed *Dancing Teepees: Poems of American Indian Youth* by Virginia Driving and Hank Sneve.

___ Read and discussed_____

___ Read and discussed_____

Asian-American and Asian Stories

Primary

___ Read and discussed *Grandfather's Journey* by Allen Say.

___ Read and discussed *A Carp for Kimiko* by Virginia Kroll.

___ Read and discussed *Aekyung's Dream* by Min Paek.

___ Read and discussed *Halmoni and the Picnic* by Sook Nyul Choi.

___ Read and discussed *Dumpling Soup* by Jamam Kim Rattigan.

___ Read and discussed *The Whispering Cloth: A Refugee's Story* by Pegi Deitz Shea.

___ Read and discussed *Onion Tears* by Diana Kidd.

___ Read and discussed_____

___ Read and discussed_____

Intermediate

___ Read and discussed *Sadako and The Thousand Paper Cranes* by Eleanor Coerr.

___ Read and discussed *Mieko and the Fifth Treasure* by Eleanor Coerr.

___ Read and discussed *The Invisible Thread* by Yoshiko Uchida.

___ Read and discussed *The Lost Garden* by Laurence Yep.

___ Read and discussed *Extraordinary Asian Pacific Americans* by Susan Sinnott.

___ Read and discussed *Elaine, Mary Lewis, and the Frogs* by Heidi Chang.

___ Read and discussed *My Best Friend Duc Tran* by Diane MacMillan and Dorothy Freeman.

___ Read and discussed_____

___ Read and discussed_____

European American and European Stories

Primary

___ Read and discussed Mother Goose rhymes.

___ Read and discussed traditional fairy tales.

___ Read and discussed *Pied Piper of Hamelin.*

___ Read and discussed *Pinocchio.*

___ Read and discussed *Rapunzel.*

___ Read and discussed *Princess and the Pea.*

___ Read and discussed *Rumpelstiltskin.*

___ Read and discussed *Snow White.*

___ Read and discussed *Ugly Duckling.*

___ Read and discussed *Sleeping Beauty*

___ Read and discussed *Alice in Wonderland.*

___ Read and discussed *Pollyanna.*

___ Read and discussed *Robinson Crusoe.*

___ Read and discussed *Paul Bunyan.*

___ Read and discussed *Pecos Bill.*

___ Read and discussed Aesop and Grimm fables.

___ Read and discussed Hans Christian Anderson fairy tales.

___ Read and discussed *The Keeping Quilt* by Patricia Polacco.

___ Read and discussed *Neve Shalom* by Laurie Dolphin.

___ Read and discussed *Make a Wish Molly* by Barbara Cohen.

___ Read and discussed *In Wintertime* by Kim Howard.

___ Read and discussed *Russian Girl: Life in a Russian Town* by Russ Kendall.

___ The *Three Princes: A Tale From the Middle East* by Eric A. Kimmel.

___ Read and discussed_____

___ Read and discussed_____

Intermediate

___ Read and discussed *Little Women* by Louisa May Alcott.

___ Read and discussed *Rip Van Winkle* and *The Legend of Sleepy Hollow* by Washington Irving.

___ Read and discussed *A Christmas Carol* by Charles Dickens.

___ Read and discussed *Treasure Island* by Robert Louis Stevenson.

___ Read and discussed *Laura Ingalls Wilder* series.

___ Read and discussed *Adventures of Tom Sawyer* by Mark Twain.

___ Read and discussed *The Diary of Anne Frank.*

___ Read and discussed *Number the Stars* by Lois Lowry.

___ Read and discussed *An Ancient Heritage: The Arab-American Minority* by Brent Ashabrannea.

___ Read and discussed *Zlata's Diary: A Child's Life in Sarajevo* by Alata Filipovic.

___ Read and discussed *A Bride for Anna's Papa* by Isabel Marvin.

___ Read and discussed_____

___ Read and discussed_____

Poetry

Poetry provides a special way to express thoughts and emotions. Experience the unique feelings that are a part of listening to poems being read aloud and by reading, writing, and memorizing them yourself. Libraries have collections of poetry on many subjects. A few famous poems are listed below.

___ Read and discussed Robert Frost's "The Road Not Taken" and "Stopping by Woods on a Snowy Evening."

___ Read and discussed Carl Sandburg's "Fog."

___ Read and discussed Joyce Kilmer's "Trees."

___ Read and discussed Emily Dickinson's "A Bird Came Down the Walk."

___ Read and discussed Edward Lawrence Thayer's "Casey at the Bat."

___ Read and discussed Henry Wadsworth Longfellow's "Song of Hiawatha" and "Paul Revere's Ride."

___ Read and discussed Langston Hughes' "Dreams."

___ Read and discussed Isaac Watts' "Against Idleness and Mischief."

■■■■■■■■■■■■■■■■■■■■■■■■■■■■■

___ Read and discussed Edward Hersey Richards' "A Wise Old Owl."

___ Read and discussed Alfred Lord Tennyson's "The Eagle."

___ Read and discussed Paul Laurence Dunbar's "Lyrics of Lowly Life."

___ Read and discussed Langston Hughes' "I, Too and Harlem."

___ Read and discussed Countee Cullen's "Incident."

___ Read and discussed Mary Austin's "A Song of Greatness."

___ Read and discussed Rebecca Caudill's "Wind, Sand and Sky."

___ Read and discussed Wade Huson's "Pass It On: African-American Poetry for Children."

___ Memorized the poem_____.

___ Memorized the poem_____.

Word Expressions

Become familiar with some of the clichés, hyperboles, and puns that are a part of the English language. Use newspapers and magazines to make a list of common expressions and their meanings.

Clichés

___ "You're barking up the wrong tree."

___ "One rotten apple can spoil the whole basket."

___ "We never miss the water till the well runs dry."

Puns

___ "We need more car pools."

___ "Her nose is running."

___ "She has a frog in her throat."

Hyperboles

___ "He laughed his head off."

___ "I'm tied up at work."

___ "I'm so hungry I could eat a horse."

SCIENCE

As you plan your order of study, keep in mind that all areas need to be studied for a broad base of scientific knowledge. Do research, experiment and observe for yourself whenever possible.

___ Experiments by asking questions, hypothesizing, doing the experiment, collecting the data, identifying patterns and relationships, interpreting and classifying the data, drawing conclusions, and asking further questions to begin the cycle again.

___ Explains how biology, zoology, botany, and ecology are connected.

___ Explains how physics, chemistry, geology, and astronomy are connected.

Life Science

Biology

___ Explains what biologists do.

___ Explains the connection between cells and the growth of plants and animals.

___ Explains the interdependent relationship of plants and animals.

___ Describes some plant and animal habitats.

___ Diagrams and explains several food chains.

___ Describes the concept of balance in nature and justifies the need for it.

■ ■

___ Explains how the population of a given species affects a natural community.

___ Explains what different living organisms need for survival.

___ Explains the relationship of heredity to genetics and chromosomes.

___ Explains why some animals and plants become endangered, and sometimes become extinct.

Zoology

___ Explains what zoologists do.

___ Compares protozoa, sponges, crustacea, and arthropods.

___ Explains the difference between vertebrates and invertebrates.

___ Classifies animals as cold-blooded, warm-blooded, amphibians, reptiles, and mammals.

___ Compares animals that are born alive with those hatched from eggs.

___ Explains why the platypus is a special kind of animal.

___ Explains how the need for food and protection is related to animal characteristics, behaviors, populations, adaptations, and size.

___ Gives examples of instinctive animal behavior.

___ Compares and contrasts migration and hibernation.

___ Explains the life cycle of several insects, including how size is related to population numbers and habitat.

___ Explains the life cycle of several animals, including how size is related to population numbers and habitat.

___ Explains the relationship between wild and domestic animals.

___ Gives examples of how animals adapt to their changing environment or become extinct.

Botany

___ Explains what botanists do.

___ Sorts and classifies plants and their seeds.

___ Gives examples of seed dispersement.

___ Explains how spores, mosses, algae, fungi, molds, and bacteria are related to each other.

___ Explains the life cycles of many plants.

___ Explains how the cycles of plant life are related to the cycles of the seasons.

___ Compares coniferous with deciduous plants, annual with perennial plants.

___ Explains how plants reproduce their own kind through flowers, seeds, and other means.

___ Explains how plants adapt to their habitat.

Ecology

___ Explains what ecologists do.

___ Identifies threats to the environment of our planet.

___ Explains why our environment has become more threatened.

___ Explains the relation between pollution and conservation.

___ Explains how population explosion can become an environmental threat.

___ Explains the connections between reduction, reuse, and recycling of resources.

___ Identifies practical means by which everyone can reduce pollution.

Physical Science

Physics

___ Explains what physicists do.

___ Explains the law of conservation of energy.

___ Diagrams and explains how light travels, and the nature of color.

___ Diagrams and explains how sound travels.

___ Explains how simple machines work such as inclined planes, wedges, pulleys, nails and screws.

___ Explains electricity and magnetism, and how to measure it.

___ Explains heat and cold and their measurement.

Chemistry

___ Explains what chemists do.

___ Explains the relationship between the three states of matter: solid, liquid, and gas.

___ Explains properties of solids, liquids, and gases.

___ Identifies compounds, elements, molecules, atoms, electrons, protons, and neutrons.

___ Explains some chemical reactions, such as the reaction of hydrogen with oxygen to produce water (H_2O).

■■■■■■■■■■■■■■■■■■■■■■■■■■■■■■■■

___ Explains the carbon and oxygen cycles in plants and animals.

___ Explains common energy sources.

Geology

___ Explains what geologists do.

___ Identifies several earth materials, and compares them with manmade materials.

___ Identifies some tests scientists use to determine the kind and age of earth materials.

___ Lists information that has been learned from fossil records.

___ Explains how fossil fuels are formed.

___ Explains how wind, fire and water change the earth's surface.

___ Explains how the Glacier Age changed the earth's surface.

___ Identifies the location of some of the earth's plates and faults, and explains how earthquakes and volcanoes are connected to them.

___ Explains the water cycle.

___ Explains the continental drift theory.

___ Diagrams what the earth would look like if it were cut in half.

Astronomy

___ Explains what astronomers do.

___ Diagrams our solar system, including distances between planets.

___ Describes the asteroid belt.

___ Explains why the weight of objects changes when they go out in space, and how this causes them to move and react differently.

___ Explains how a compass works.

___ Explains how gravity affects planets and moons.

___ Explains how gravity creates the ocean tide.

___ Explains the relationship of galaxies to stars.

___ Identifies several constellations.

___ Explains how atmospheric conditions affect climate and weather.

___ Explains why the earth's atmosphere helps to sustain life on our planet.

Important Scientists

Learn why some scientists are famous. Write the reasons for which they are remembered and add more names to this list.

Charles Babbage _____

Benjamin Banneker_____

Clara Barton _____

Alexander Graham Bell _____

Elizabeth Blackwell_____

Rachel Carson _____

George Washington Carver _____

Nicolaus Copernicus_____

Marie Curie _____

Charles Darwin _____

Charles Drew_____

Albert Einstein_____

Thomas Edison _____

Alexander Fleming _____

Benjamin Franklin_____

Galileo Galilei_____

Jane Goodall_____

Mae Jemison_____

Anton van Leeuwenhoek_____

Ada Lovelace _____

Elijah McCoy _____

Gregor Mendel_____

Samuel F. B. Morse _____

Isaac Newton _____

Daniel Hale Williams _____

Wilbur and Orville Wright_____

HEALTH AND PHYSICAL FITNESS

___ Explains the difference between nutritious and non-nutritious foods.

___ Explains importance of vitamins and minerals in nutrition.

___ Explains how food choices affect health and lifestyle.

___ Eats healthy foods and snacks.

___ Explains how exercise and leisure time sports are important to physical fitness and personal enjoyment.

___ Participates regularly in vigorous physical activity or leisure time sports.

___ Explains what to do to stay safe at home, at school, on the bus, and out in the community.

___ Explains what to do in case of fire, poisoning, accidents, and other emergencies.

___ Explains how to take care of ears, eyes, and teeth.

___ Takes proper care of ears, eyes, and teeth.

___ Explains things to do to prevent the spread of communicable diseases.

___ Explains safe and unsafe uses of chemicals and drugs.

___ Identifies some unsafe chemicals and drugs, and how their use affect oneself and family.

___ Explains the body's skeletal, muscular, respiratory, cardiovascular, nervous, and digestive systems and how they work together.

■ ■

Human Relations

___ Explains why it is important to learn to work with others and be physically and verbally considerate.

___ Explains several methods for resolving conflicts.

___ Explains how to maintain friendships and support diversity.

___ Explains why it is important to assume different roles when working on group projects: leader, recorder, time keeper, and praiser.

___ Communicates effectively with others.

___ Works successfully with others on projects and during leisure time.

___ Explains good methods for solving personal problems, which include evaluating consequences of various choices.

___ Explains ways to handle stress and criticism.

___ Takes pride in oneself and work.

___ Appreciates the unique qualities of oneself.

___ Appreciates the diversity seen in others and displays value, care, and compassion for others.

___ Volunteers service to the community.

Add to your expertise of ways to solve conflicts peacefully by reading books that deal with conflict resolution. A few of those books are listed below, from easiest to hardest.

___ *The Pain and the Great One* by Judy Blume

___ *The Fight* by Betty Boegehold

___ *Bailey the Big Bully* by Liz Boyd

___ *Best Friends* by Steven Kellogg

___ *Peace on the Playground* by Eileen Lucas

___ *A Visit to Amy-Claire* by Claudia Mills

___ *Ruby the Copycat* by Peggy Rathmann

___ *Peace Begins With You* by Katherine Scholes

___ *Third Grade Is Terrible* by Barbara Baker

___ *Strider* by Beverly Cleary

___ *Best Friends Club* by Elizabeth Withrop

___ *The Art Lesson* by Tomie dePoala

___ *Aldo Peanut Butter* by Johanna Hurwitz

___ *Desperate for a Dog* by Rosa Impey

___ *Twenty Ways to Lose Your Best Friend* by Marilyn Singer

___ *Fourth Grade Rats* by Jerry Spinelli

___ *Randall's Wall* by Carol Fenner

___ *The Practical Joke War* by Alane Ferguson

___ *The Queen of Put-Down* by Nancy Hopper

___ *Shiloh* by Phillis Reynolds Naylor

___ *Reluctantly Alice* by Phillis Reynolds Naylor

___ *The Pennywhistle Tree* by Doris Buchanan Smith

___ *Wonder* by Rachel Vail

■■■■■■■■■■■■■■■■■■■■■■■■■■■

CULTURE, GOVERNMENT, AND ECONOMICS

___ Explains why government is necessary and important.

___ Identifies the values and principles of our culturally diverse democratic form of government

___ Explains how world interdependence affects our own government and culture.

___ Explains how the three branches of government work together in a system of check and balance system.

___ Explains the value of having political parties.

___ Explains fair representation.

___ Describes how our form of government depends on responsible citizens making competent decisions for the common good of society.

___ Compares our democracy with other forms of government.

___ Explains how nations interact with each other.

___ Identifies patriotic symbols and songs.

___ Compares basic beliefs of the world religions of Judaism, Christianity, Islam, Hinduism, Buddhism, and Confucianism.

___ Explains why we are globally interdependent, and why conflicts quickly become global concerns today.

___ Compares the great movements of people between countries that have taken place both recently and long ago.

___ Explains how scarcity and choice, needs and wants, influence our economic decisions.

___ Explains how our own present buying and selling choices impact what our future buying opportunities will be.

■ ■

___ Explains how our economic choices affect us, our community, country, and world.

Historical Events

Take an interest in the following historical events and be able to tell why each is significant.

North and South America

___ Land bridge from Asia and North America's first civilization

___ Anasazi people of Mesa Verde, Colorado

___ Inca civilization of South America

___ English settlement of North America; Pilgrims, slavery

___ American Revolution and Declaration of Independence

___ U.S. Constitution and Bill of Rights

___ Presidents George Washington and Thomas Jefferson

___ Louisiana Purchase of 1803

___ War of 1812

___ Simon Bolivar of South America

___ American Indian cultures and history, wars and reservations

___ Annexation of Texas in 1845, Mexican War, and Treaty of 1848

___ Oregon Territory and Treaty with Great Britain of 1846

___ The California Gold Rush

___ Abraham Lincoln, Civil War and abolition of slavery

___ Transcontinental railroad

___ Industrial Age of Capitalists and monopolies

___ Industrial Revolution, laissez-faire policy, capitalism and socialism

___ Ellis Island and the Great Immigration

___ Spanish-American War, Cuba, and the Philippines

___ Conservation programs and reforms of Theodore Roosevelt

___ First World War

___ The Great Depression and Franklin Roosevelt

___ Second World War, Japanese internment camps, and atomic bomb

___ The Korean War

___ Civil Rights Movement and Martin Luther King Jr.

___ Cuban Missile Crisis and Cuban Refugees

___ The Vietnam War and the Vietnamese boat people

___ The Feminist Movement

___ Space exploration and moon landings

Europe

___ The Greeks and the Romans

___ Dark Ages, feudalism, and Catholic Church

___ European Renaissance and the Protestant Reformation

___ The French Revolution and Napoleon

___ Russian Revolution, Lenin and Stalin

___ Rise and fall of the British empire

___ World War I

___ Hitler and World War II

___ Communism and the Berlin Wall

Africa and Asia

___ Egypt and the Nile

___ The Persians and Babylonians

___ Hebrews and Israel

___ Rise of African Empires and trade

___ European rule of Africa and apartheid

___ Development of Chinese culture

___ Development of Indian culture

___ Development of Japanese culture

___ European contacts with China and Japan

___ China's Opium War and Boxer Rebellion

___ Japan's modernization and World War II

___ Chinese Revolution and Communism

___ Rise of independent nations and economic development

Famous People

Know why some historically famous people are remembered. Add to the following list.

Authors

___ Louisa May Alcott   _____

___ Pearl Buck   _____

___ Emily Dickinson   _____

___ Helen Keller   _____

___ Ida B. Wells   _____

Educators

___ Mary McLeod Bethune   _____

___ Horace Mann   _____

___ Booker T. Washington   _____

Civil Rights Leaders

___ Cesar Chavez   _____

___ Prudence Crandall   _____

___ W.E.B. Du Bois   _____

___ Frederick Douglass   _____

___ Marian Wright Edelman   _____

___ Marcus Garvey   _____

___ Martin Luther King, Jr.   _____

___ Malcolm X   _____

___ Rosa Parks   _____

___ A. Philip Randolph   _____

___ Sojourner Truth   _____

___ Harriet Tubman   _____

Women's Rights Leaders

___ Susan B. Anthony   _____

___ Amelia Bloomer   _____

___ Lucretia Mott   _____

___ Elizabeth Mott   _____

___ Elizabeth Cady Stanton   _____

Social Reformers

___ Jane Adams   _____

___ Dorothea Dix   _____

___ Eleanor Roosevelt   _____

Indian Leaders

___ Geronimo   _____

___ Osceola   _____

___ Pontiac   _____

___ Sitting Bull   _____

___ Sequoyah   _____

Explorers

___ Richard E. Byrd   _____

___ John Cabot   _____

___ Jacques Cartier   _____

___ Christopher Columbus   _____

___ Hernan Cortes   _____

___ Vasco da Gama   _____

___ Henry Hudson   _____

___ David Livingstone   _____

___ Ferdinand Magellan   _____

___ Francisco Pizarro   _____

___ Robert Peary   _____

___ Walter Raleigh   _____

___ Sacagawea   _____

Inventors

___ Thomas Edison   _____

___ Henry Ford   _____

___ Robert Fulton   _____

___ Robert Goddard   _____

___ Guglielmo Marconi   _____

FINE ARTS

Visual Arts

___ Views artwork displays representing different cultures and compares and contrasts them.

___ Creates art products using a variety of techniques and media.

___ Identifies some elements of art used to communicate an idea or emotion.

___ Explains the relationship between the primary, secondary, and tertiary colors.

___ Explains how to mix tints and shades, and the effects each gives.

___ Compares the feelings associated with "warm" colors with those of "cool" colors.

___ Explains how symmetry and patterns are used in art.

___ Explains methods to create perspective, depth, and the illusion of light.

___ Explains why buildings like cathedrals, castles, domes, mosques and shrines are considered works of art.

___ Identifies many different forms of art observable in daily life.

Famous Artists and Artwork

Learn about these famous artists and cultural forms of art. Compare the artwork of different cultures and historical time periods. Add to those listed below.

___ Leonardo da Vinci _____

___ Winslow Homer _____

___ Edward Hopper _____

___ Michelangelo _____

___ Claude Monet _____

___ Edvard Munch _____

___ Pablo Picasso _____

___ Raphael _____

___ Rembrandt _____

___ Diego Rivera _____

___ Auguste Rodin _____

___ Henry O. Tanner _____

___ Grant Wood _____

___ Andrew Wyeth _____

___ Vincent van Gogh _____

___ Jan Van Eyck _____

___ Native American artwork _____

___ African artwork _____

___ Asian artwork _____

___ South American artwork _____

Performing Arts

Music

___ Works with others in a group to create or produce music.

___ Identifies the letter names of the lines and spaces of the treble staff.

▪ ■ ▪ ■ ▪ ■ ▪ ■ ▪ ■ ▪ ■ ▪ ■ ▪ ■ ▪ ■ ▪ ■ ▪ ■ ▪ ■ ▪ ■

___ Explains how sharps and flats affect musical notes.

___ Defines, explains, or demonstrates scale, octave, meter, and tempo in music.

___ Identifies music phrases.

___ Identifies patterns in music.

___ Explains rounds or canons.

___ Identifies some sound differences between instruments of the orchestra, as well as instruments from around the world.

___ Sings with correct posture and intonation.

___ Sings or plays major and minor scales.

___ Reads or performs rhythms and chants using common note values.

___ Maintains a steady beat for playing percussion instruments.

___ Plays instruments such as a xylophone, autoharp, and recorder.

___ Compares baroque, romantic, and modern forms of music.

___ Compares global styles of music such as Middle Eastern, Far Eastern, African, and Native American.

Famous Musicians

Learn about famous musicians and what their music tells us about their time period and culture.

Mozart, classical Austrian-German _____

Beethoven, classical German_____

Bach, baroque German_____

Handel, baroque English _____

John Philip Sousa, romantic American_____

Louis Armstrong, modern African-American jazz_____

Scott Joplin, modern African-American ragtime _____

Stravinsky, modern Russian-American _____

Libby Larson, modern American (Minnesota) _____

Heiter Villa-Lobos, Brazilian _____

B B King, blues African-American _____

Francis Scott Key, national anthem_____

Drama and Dance

___ Views drama and dance productions, and critiques them.

___ Explains the difference between comedy and tragedy in drama.

___ Compares folk dancing with ballet and tap dancing.

THINKING AND LEARNING SKILLS

___ Asks questions about the surrounding world.

___ Imagines how a person, place, or thing could be different.

___ Seeks additional information to satisfy curiosity.

___ Explains steps to take to arrive at a good solution to a problem or a creative answer to a question.

___ Explains how to approach problems by thinking of many unusual and creative solutions, considering their consequences and predicting outcomes, and placing them in some order of priority.

___ Explains how to be creative by adding or subtracting an element, making some part smaller or larger, or rearranging the parts.

___ Avoids choosing solutions or drawing conclusions too quickly, and can explain why it is important to defer judgment.

___ Compares similarities and differences of situations or with problems trying to understand them.

___ Transfers learning from one experience or observation to another.

___ Uses precise language when explaining information.

___ Checks answers for accuracy.

___ Takes enough time to understand a situation sufficiently well.

___ Identifies major sources of information.

___ Uses computers and modems to access, organize and communicate information.

___ Explains how the many forms of modern technology have changed the way we live and work.

___ Explains the possible consequences for searching out indecent information and choosing indecent television and computer program exposure.

CHAPTER 3

PARENTS, WHAT ARE YOUR RESPONSIBILITIES?

PARENT: *"The neighbors are here. Turn off the TV so we can talk."*
Children: *"Please, just let us watch one more program!"*

The children settle in front of the television set with parents on chairs nearby. Two hours later everyone is watching yet another program.

Mother: *"I don't know how the schools manage to teach kids anything these days. I only hope our kids are getting a good education."*

Father: *"I know I should be doing more to help my kids learn, but I have my own work to do and I need time just to relax."*

Be their best teacher.

Parents, you greatly influence what and how your children learn. If you do not teach them, you permit them to learn about the world through television, friends, and other means you cannot control. Today, more than ever, children are tempted to become passive observers who simply consume, rather than active evaluative thinkers who enjoy contributing to society.

PARENTS SHAPE SCHOOL SUCCESS

■ ■

Your children need you to be their best teacher. You are responsible for all of their out-of-classroom learning time, including the appropriate use of computers and television. Your choices shape the learning of concepts and values during this time which, in turn, impact what they learn when they are in the classroom.

Without your supportive teaching, children find it easy to neglect educational pursuits in favor of here-and-now pleasures. This aversion to academic learning reduces even further their interest in it. On the other hand, when they succeed as a result of your teaching, they seek further successes that open surprising new doors of opportunity.

Resources now available enable you to do a better job of teaching your children than ever before. A computer with a modem and connection with the Internet can instantly bring words and pictures about science, nature, new discoveries, world events, and the arts to you. Through electronic bulletin boards you can exchange ideas with other children and adults around the world. Some families even set up their own home pages on the World Wide Web and invite "visitors" to drop in. Families who lack computers of their own can access these in an increasing number of public schools and libraries.

You can find other resources in museums, art galleries, and nature centers to supplement the abundance of books. Check with these to get a schedule of classes and tours especially designed for elementary-age children. You as a parent may also help these institutions as a volunteer and get free access to them, besides providing a good example of community service to your children.

Have a plan.

Parent: *"What shall we write in your baby book today?"*

As the parents talk they record the day's happenings.

Parent: *"You're now a month old, and we have big plans for you."*

As parents, when you begin one of life's most demanding tasks, raising a child, you make careful plans and record information in baby books. As your children grow, however, it is easy to stop recording information and neglect the lofty goals.

Most worthwhile accomplishments come from following written plans. They help you record progress and celebrate achievements. With them you can chart the course and direction you want to move. Even with an older child, you can gain the advantages of planning by starting now.

The learning plan in this book outlines such a road map for you. It guides you to select the activities and opportunities for learning that help your children to make steady progress.

Following a structured educational program, your choices and involvement in whatever you do will be purposeful and worthwhile. It enables you to counter time and peer pressures that would otherwise sidetrack you. You can also evaluate television viewing and other leisure activities for their contribution to the educational plan.

Individualize the plan.

The father and grandfather of twins watch them as they play checkers.

Father: *"They don't even seem like sisters."*

Grandfather: *"They look alike but they are so different from each other."*

Every child should experience the joy of being unique and special. Your educational plans should reflect this difference. Some children enjoy pursuing one area of study in great depth, while others like covering many topics quickly. There are those who find it difficult to concentrate for any sustained period of time. Some learn primarily from what they see and others from what they hear. One child is musically inclined, and another likes to draw and paint.

Your learning **programs should be customized** for each of your children. To gain understanding, you need to spend time with them. Listen to what they say and be sensitive to their special talents and limitations.

Notice how individual differences manifest themselves in work habits, ways of looking at things, and patterns of thought. They appear in products like artwork and creative writing. Always value and encourage such uniqueness and creativity. You do this by allowing them to make choices, encouraging fantasy, providing for openness and flexibility, and showing that you trust them.

The specific plans you develop, however, should include the mastering of basic skills which all children need, such as learning to read, write, and do math well. Even very unique children need these. You may have to discover special ways to make these essential concepts clear and understandable. Some need more time than others to learn a given concept, and you will need to be understanding.

Emphasize good work skills.

Father: *"I don't know why it takes our son so long to do a simple little job."*

Mother: *"He certainly spends a lot of energy trying to avoid having to do something. Maybe that's just the way he is."*

We often assume that children learn good work skills on their own, and that any difficulties they have are due to unique physical or character traits. However, most children can learn them if they are deliberately taught. Without these skills, even well-designed educational plans can fail.

From the beginning, teach your children to **complete simple tasks well**, with allowances for individual differences in ability and work speed. They need to know how to complete high-quality work in an appropriate amount of time. Together with your children, estimate the time needed to complete various tasks, record the actual time they spend on it, and decide how to improve work habits. Help them realize that if they complete a task well, they will have more opportunities for other pursuits they enjoy.

In today's information age, everyone should be able to quickly scan material and know when and how to read some of it carefully. Thus, you should occasionally check to see that they are **varying their reading speed** to suit the material they have and what they want to learn from it. Also help them to be able to read aloud fluently, with appropriate speed and expression.

Teach your children while young to **learn from their mistakes.** Help them to always be open to better ways of doing things. Analyze errors with them and plan how to improve. Above all, don't make them feel guilty or incompetent because of their mistakes. Rather, view them as learning opportunities.

Prepare your children to **be skilled communicators.** Encourage them, as they gather and share information from research, so that they feel comfort and competence in their proficiency to both write and speak. Provide experiences that develop their ability to know when to listen, when to speak, and how to respond to others' questions and ideas.

Value a good education.

Daughter: *"Everyone liked my presentation! I knew you'd be happy to hear that."*

Father: *"Great! We are pleased with how well you are doing at school. Being able to do excellent work on assignments is very important. You must feel good about your ability to complete projects."*

Children develop a motivation to learn when you as the parent make learning a priority in your family and impress on your children that what they are learning is important. Gradually, as your children excel in learning, the **inner satisfaction and enjoyment** they receive enables them to work hard and persist on their own.

When your children know that you value education they will feel that they should be good learners. **You need not be well-educated yourself.** Many of the immigrants who have come to our country lacked good schooling opportunities, yet they have convinced their children of the value of education which has enabled them to rise to the top in our schools.

You need to communicate by your own example that learning is important. Otherwise, your children will believe what they see you do rather than what they hear you say. If you want your children to enjoy learning, you need to express your own enjoyment as you continually learn yourself. If you expect your children to make good educational choices, then you need to lead an exemplary lifestyle.

For example, if you read challenging books in your spare time and discussing what you learn with them, they will realize that reading is important. Your adult conversations on serious issues can model a thinking process which they will adopt as they grow up. On the other hand, it will be difficult for children to accept your teaching about something like choosing nutritious foods if you consume lots of junk food yourself.

Make home a conducive place for learning.

Child: *"Where's my homework? The bus is coming!"*

Parent: *"Oh no! You didn't get your homework finished! And where is that overdue library book?"*

Child: *"And today is the last day to bring my field trip permission slip!"*

Children learn how to work and keep things organized by observing you in the process of living and seeing how you manage your home. When you **provide an organized environment with a good stock of supplies**, they value working and keeping things neat themselves.

Each of your children need to have her or his own learning area with shelves and a lamp, and to know how to keep it organized. Some essential supplies are pens, pencils, erasers, crayons, markers, watercolors, lots of paper, notebooks, envelopes, stamps, and reference books. Younger children need simple, safe supplies which allow them to explore and solve problems, observe and interact, without the threat of doing things wrong. Older students need a dictionary, thesaurus, atlas, and calculator.

Supplies need not be expensive. Sometimes businesses give away recyclable paper. You can encourage relatives and friends to give gifts of educational supplies. Libraries have information on how to send for free materials on all kinds of subjects. Your children can write for them and send "thank you" notes as part of their learning experiences.

Plan for display areas in your home where your children can put up good work to be shared and praised. Help them to send their best writings and artwork to children's magazines for publication—check with your school or library for their names and addresses.

Schedule times for both quiet study and conversation so each is important to them. Everyone should enjoy taking an active part in the talking times. All should feel comfortable making positive statements about each other and in graciously accepting compliments. You can show them how to appropriately express their own concerns and their compassion for others. In your conversations you can also share delightful and amusing situations from daily life and plan creative activities to do together.

Create a thinking atmosphere. Encourage discussions on differing points of view. Play thinking games like creating stories involving random objects around the room. Give as much importance to thinking of interesting and provocative questions as to giving answers to them.

Extend Learning Outside the Home.

Child: *"First, Grandma and Grandpa took us to this huge park with all kinds of slides! Then we ate our lunch in another park and fed the birds. And after that, we went to the museum!"*

Fortunate are the children who have a community of educators to help them. There is so much for children to learn, and you as a parent have your own economic and social demands which limit your time and energy. Grandparents, siblings, and other responsible relatives and caretakers can enrich your children's lives by sharing in their education.

Although you should clearly be in charge and use only reliable people, extending learning outside of the home can **foster a spirit of resourcefulness within your children and provide for many more learning opportunities**. Multiple experiences help children to be independent, accept parenting from several adults, and learn to get along with different kinds of people.

When caretaking is shared and the community is used, children have access to a wealth of learning resources. They can turn to librarians for advice on reading and using the Internet. Scientists at museums, nature centers, zoos, and planetariums can share knowledge that goes beyond what you as parents can provide. An artist at a local gallery can tell them about colors and designs, and convince them that they can enjoy creating their own art.

Actively support your local community.

Child: *"I can't come over tonight. I have a lot of things to do. I'm helping my parents so they have time to be scout leaders."*

Friend: *"Maybe I should do that too. Then my parents could help our 4-H club."*

A wide variety of programs like the scouts, athletic events, and church programs in your community are made available because people volunteer their time. **Take advantage of these programs, but also carefully plan to give back to your local community.** You can be a club leader, program director, or serve on a local committee or governing board. You can volunteer to direct an event, contribute supplies to an activity, or send family notes of appreciation. If nothing else, you can contribute money which many of these programs are usually short of.

When you volunteer service to the community your children can better appreciate the other adults who make their out-of-school programs possible. As a family, plan your own special community service projects like picking up litter and recycling wastes. Involvement in these activities will teach your children to help make our world a better place for everyone.

Support public schools.

Parent: *"When my child is old enough I'm not sending him to a public school. So many people complain about the awful job the public schools are doing."*

Neighbor: *"All of my children went to public schools. They got a good education. Many schools do an excellent job of teaching our children. They have very dedicated teaching staffs. I think that we need to support schools more as well as find ways to make them better."*

Our democratic form of government provides for equal educational opportunities through its school system. When we help all children to be well educated we enable them to become successful contributing workers and community members. By so doing we fight violence and crime, and make life better for ourselves as well.

All citizens can voice respect for our public educational institutions. Wherever your children receive their schooling, you as parents can contribute services and supplies to the public schools in your area. You can encourage the teachers by voicing support, sending notes, and attending school events. You can study the issues and vote for the people and educational measures that support public schools.

Be a good model.

Child: *"What are you doing?"*

Friend: *"I'm making a surprise gift for someone who is sick. That's what my mother is always doing!"*

Children remember best what they see and experience. You are your children's strongest role models. Therefore, you must **set the example** for what you want your children to do and be. If you want them to be kind and thoughtful, you must reflect kindness in what you do and say. If you want them to listen to you, you must also listen to what they are saying.

If you want your children to be constructive thinkers, you need to share your thoughts with them as together you evaluate situations, verify information, seek logical evidence, and solve problems. If you want them to be independent thinkers, you must model it in how you respond to what they say and think. Whether it be in attitudes, skills, or communication, you need to be a exemplary model for your children.

Be positive and show compassion.

Parent: *"I know I'm right. Then why do you always disagree with me?"*

Parent: *"You're the one who always starts the arguments. And then you start yelling!"*

When the adults in a home are frequently angry and critical, children can develop undesirable perceptions of themselves and other people. They can become irritable themselves and, in turn, be disruptive and aggressive. Your children may do the opposite of what you teach when you display negative attitudes.

On the other hand, children who are treated with warmth and support develop confidence in their ability to do things. A child who has an optimistic attitude is much more likely to be successful.

Therefore, you need to **model and nurture positive outlooks**, "I can do it" attitudes. Learn to enjoy overcoming difficulties together. Develop respect for your differences, and help each other to deal with criticism and failure. Don't be afraid to explain that you too make mistakes, and that you can learn to avoid them afterward.

You need to **be compassionate and sympathetic,** expecting your children's best but not perfection. This requires much patience. You can clear up misunderstandings by paraphrasing one another's statements to see whether you understood their meaning. When conflicts do arise, stop, reevaluate, and plan ways to resolve them.

Praise promotes good feelings. Use it frequently, sincerely and specifically where it is deserved. Take care to keep eye contact with your children so you can read their nonverbal signals as well as listen to their words. Respond to their messages in a way that encourages them to be open to you.

Even criticism can be given in a positive manner. Together discuss difficulties as opportunities to learn. Assist with the smaller steps that aid in reaching a goal. Often reassure each of your children of your genuine love for them as very special persons, and separate it from what they do and say. When criticizing, take care to recognize and praise even the smallest positive attainments.

Too firm a demand for obedience can discourage compassion and curiosity. Remember, it is the little subtleties that make all the difference!

Spend time talking.

Child: *"I wonder what my parents would say if I told them?"*

Friend: *"Mine would wait a few seconds and then they would have just the right words for an answer."*

Your children learn communication skills by listening to you talk and by observing you listen to them. By talking they learn to organize their thoughts and express ideas clearly and precisely. Today's most needed thinking skills are best developed through expressing thoughts and hearing how they sound to others.

Yet, many families do not spend much time conversing. They have busy schedules and rarely enjoy mealtime conversations. Some families even prefer watching television to talking at mealtimes. They don't feel comfortable sharing their daily experiences and feelings.

Teachers understand the importance of spending time talking, but they have time constraints. Relatives and friends are often too busy as well.

Therefore, you must **plan for family discussion times**. Whether these occasions include eating or not, they need to be regular opportunities for family members to sit down and engage in give-and-take dialogues. Share the leadership with your children and help everyone to feel comfortable asking questions and working through issues.

Maintain an atmosphere of respect and support so your children can modify their thinking structures as they assimilate new information and learn appropriate and accurate thought processes. Give them opportunities to express information, defend a point of view, and modify their opinions.

By developing these skills through spending time talking, you can also build family cohesiveness. Conversing can help your children to feel valued and loved, and counter peer pressures to deviate from your values.

CHAPTER 4

WHAT ARE THE STUDENT'S RESPONSIBILITIES?

M AKE Good Choices.

You can try to teach your children how to make good choices, model good choosing for them, and provide appropriate learning experiences, but ultimately they must decide for themselves.

You best assure success by **beginning early** and by recognizing the small accomplishments. **Praise them frequently** for keeping their work space organized and contributing to household chores. Thank them for being on time and being polite. Continually write them notes of appreciation on napkins or taped to the refrigerator.

Chart and evaluate progress with them on difficult skills or work schedules. Use graphs to get a concrete picture of what took place and decide the next steps together. It is usually helpful to learn to do the most difficult and important tasks first, and not procrastinate.

Discuss the seriousness of choices, including television and computer program choices. Children need to know that choices always have consequences, whether pleasant or painful. The power to make choices also means accepting responsibility for the results, even if they didn't anticipate or want them.

Defer gratification.

Children need to learn to choose long term rewards over instant gratification if they are to be good self-managers in our pleasure-driven society. Recognize that they can be discouraged when they see other children choose immediate and easy things and seem to have more fun.

As a family, **set long term goals,** take the little steps necessary to reach them, and **celebrate** the joys of deferring gratification for the more worthwhile accomplishments. Then help your children set their individual long term goals. Work with them to keep their deferred gratification clearly in focus, to anticipate the positive results, and to evaluate the long range benefits derived from developing this ability.

Keep in mind that something like saving money for next year's week at camp, or choosing only essential clothes, can be challenging when others are spending their money on the latest toys or fad clothes. Therefore, work together with your children and be sure that you also do not do such things as spend money irresponsibly.

Show appreciation.

Children need to learn to appreciate all that others do for them and give to them. Failure to do so can prevent the development of warm relationships with others and decrease opportunities for learning.

Have your children **thank all their caregivers** regularly by writing notes, drawing pictures, and gathering flowers. They can also express thanks over the phone, at the dinner table or at any time of contact.

Be Responsible.

Ultimately, learning to be responsible or the failure to do so determines what a person becomes and accomplishes.

Children show that they are responsible when they independently complete expected tasks well. They learn this **by completing small expectations over an extended period of time** until they can be trusted to always do them correctly. They become more responsible as they gradually learn to take charge of themselves and consistently do what is right.

Being responsible includes accepting and enjoying being oneself, and helping others to do the same. It involves showing respect for others and the environment, and rejecting physical or verbal violence as a means of solving conflicts.

CHAPTER 5

WHAT ARE THE SCHOOL'S RESPONSIBILITIES?

PRECISELY **describe the services they offer.**
Just what should our schools be doing? How should they be run and what should they teach? This has sparked great debates and much legislation for decades. Many citizens, educators among them, still do not have a clear picture of what are the best and most realistic expectations of schools for the limited amounts of time teachers have to spend with large groups of students. There are no clear solutions for the many problems that confront schools today.

Lofty expectations have come forward and many reforms have been tried only to be dropped before their results can be fully evaluated. Schools keep changing programs, materials, and expectations. When finances get tight, administrators cut new programs and start other ones later.

Through it all, you can be left with an unclear picture of just what your children are being taught and who is deciding it. Besides general information, often you must rely on assessment reports of past happenings that suggest success or the lack of it to you. These report card and portfolio evaluations are themselves hard to interpret.

The questions remain. What should they learn and what did they learn? Do methods and practices "blur" what is being studied and achieved? What does the grade on the report card really mean? Is the work in the portfolio an honest representation of what your child can do today without help, or what they did once with help?

Yet, today you need a clear picture and precise information. Without knowing what your children will learn at school, it can be difficult to manage out-of-school learning. You will need to **request** that schools precisely describe the services they offer, and **work with the information they do provide.**

Offer what they are in the best position to teach.

Our society seems to be slow in recognizing that schools cannot teach everything. We must encourage schools to **teach well what they are best prepared to do, and put greater effort into supporting parents** in assuming their educational responsibilities.

If many academic skills can be learned, or at least enriched, away from the classroom, then schools can put more time into teaching such things as social and group skills that they can better facilitate. For example, it may be easier for parents to teach some of the math and reading skills at home with the help of a computer and recognize that schools are better places than homes to debate issues and learn specialized music and art skills.

It remains to be seen how much **schools will change** in the future. The possibilities seem limitless: educational experiences guided by individual learning plans like the one in this book, specific choices of topics for study and attendance times linked to such plans, classes to help parents teach, more community involvement and support, improved use of technology, realistic neighborhood problem-solving projects, and evening parent-child classes. New electronic technologies for linking schools with homes and libraries will come as they are affordable.

Do not allow schools to become entertainment centers.

Today's teachers are confronted with many students who just want to have fun. Our material-oriented society encourages constant pleasure-seeking. There's television to watch, computer games to play, and the latest gadgets to buy.

Children come to school wanting fun and, without instant gratification, many of them distract the learning of others. It is easy to spend a disproportionate amount of classroom time watching television and playing computer games. With the present emphasis on student rights, schools can become more like entertainment centers. Students lose further learning time with other unessential, but entertaining, school programs and activities.

Teachers and principals need to **help children to grasp the long-term benefits of hard work and serious study, and keep undesirable peer influence at a minimum.** They must particularly resist the temptation to win the short-run favor of students by making schools simply enjoyable, forfeiting the "real world" purposes for which society pays their salaries.

**Assist parents in taking an active
role in their children's education.**

Schools need to acknowledge their limits and maximize the important role the parents play as the children's most continuous teacher. They need to honestly describe their teaching plans and keep parents informed.

Although teachers can lend support and advice to parents, a teacher's time is very limited. Schools need to **provide classes in competent parenting, and assign specific staff members to assist parents with their teaching roles.**

CHAPTER 6

WHAT SHOULD THE COMMUNITY PROVIDE?

MAINTAIN **public schools and services.**
Our country has a long history of endeavoring to provide equal educational opportunities for all of its children, unlike many other countries. By educating all we believe we provide a better future for the whole nation.

Along with police and fire services, parks, recreation, transportation, and other public services, communities provide places for learning. These public schools **give the young the opportunity for access to jobs in the future.**

Schools do not exist in isolation, however. They are a major asset to a healthy community. As an economic resource they attract businesses, because families want to live there. They give the community a sense of identity, provide a place for people to gather, and offer a center for cultural events.

Good **schools and communities are interdependent**, each contributing to the well-being of the other. Esteemed communities become nurturing places for healthy families. Stable homes in turn help the schools to be outstanding learning places.

As communities and schools work together they develop public spirit. Families are then motivated to act spontaneously in the best interests of all. Parents help educate children. Every person who teaches and learns becomes a resource for the community.

Connect students with the real world of work.

Along with their learning, children ought to see where adults work and what it is like. **They need to understand the relationships between what they are studying and the world of work.** This is essential in their comprehension of why they must develop good technical, collaborative, and problem-solving skills.

In many places, businesses, service groups, and parents actively build these connections between school and work. As resource people, some have groups or individuals come to their workplace and they demonstrate needed job skills. Others go to the schools to promote career awareness and share practical uses for the skills children are learning.

Some schools provide teachers with lists of community workers and the specific subject area to which they are best prepared to contribute. Almost all of the adults in a community have specific skills which they can beneficially relate to classroom learning.

Provide activities that extend and enrich school learning.

Most communities demonstrate that they value and support education by providing activities to stretch and enhance learning during children's out-of-school time. They **sponsor classes** in the arts and crafts, sports, computer skills, and many other valuable subjects. Parents can find listings of these in the local newspaper, public libraries, and the schools themselves.

Many local community leaders are actively **seeking creative solutions in supporting families and learning** today. Some have enlarged school gyms and made them into community recreation and learning facilities for after school hours and weekends. People are taught to be good citizens as they learn about physical fitness and sportsmanship.

Families also undertake a wide variety of collaborative efforts. They range from building elaborate playgrounds for after school use to establishing neighborhood block clubs that provide for safety and family inclusiveness.

Yet, there is **much more that can be done**. The learning environments in most communities today are being challenged by social changes that have occurred in our culture. People are now more loosely bound together and transient, more pleasure-seeking, and more materially-oriented. Adults divorce easily, neglect and abuse children and each other, and are less neighborly. The gap is widening between the rich and the poor in many cities.

Communities need to establish more programs that help to resolve these social problems. We cannot expect schools, even with their staffs of psychologists and social workers, to deal with all the issues that today's families are unable to handle.

CHAPTER 7

THE REAL WORLD OF PUBLIC SCHOOLS

IF you choose to use public schools, you will want to learn as much as you can about their services and how best to work together with them. Some states and school districts now permit you to choose between two or more public schools, rather than require attendance at one specific school.

How do I choose a good school?

As you shop for a school, **look for solid academic teaching, high expectations for students, and a dedicated school staff. Observe the school in action at different times** during the day and year. Talk with members of the staff and student body to get a variety of views and experiences. Look for a clean, safe, stimulating atmosphere with a democratic decision-making structure. Notice if students are involved in high quality creative projects.

Try to find a school **where teachers endeavor to build group cohesiveness and foster a sense of community**. Children spend a lot of time at school. All should experience being part of a group where every person is valued and has friends within the group. It can be difficult for children to make friends and feel a part of a class when they are repeatedly sorted into groups with different teachers.

Ask how long students spend with their homeroom teacher and what is done to build group support. Even young children can be taught to manage their class environment efficiently and fairly. They can democratically decide such things as which projects they want to do or how to spend their party money and time. Students can learn to manage their recess time peacefully, taking care to include everyone in activities. Look for signs that show that students help each other learn, and express appreciation for what they produce together and as individuals.

There are other specifics you need to ask about. Does the school include children from diverse cultural and socioeconomic backgrounds which provide a richer background for learning citizenship? Will you receive accurate, precise, and timely progress reports? How many students are assigned to each class and what kind of support services are provided for teachers?

Check on how subjects are taught. Math and science should include real life problems and hands-on experiences. See that history is taught in such a way that it helps students to better understand and be contributing members of the present world. It is best to have the teaching of thinking skills included in most subject areas.

The reading of myths, legends, and fairy tales ought to add to children's understanding of various histories and cultures. Biographies and other forms of literature should be helping them to better understand time concepts and our common humanity.

Find out if students are taught to express their emotions in peaceful and nonjudgmental ways. See if as much emphasis is given to students' responsibilities as to their rights. Notice if students work comfortably in groups, as well as independently at their own pace.

Be alert to the way schools regard parents. Some will treat you as a passive audience or want to exclude you entirely, while others consider you an active participant in your child's educational experiences. **Look for places where teachers will actively support you in your role as a teacher at home**.

Beyond this, you need to think of the larger picture when considering school choice. Today's star schools may not be the best ones tomorrow. The quality of a school can change even from year to year, as teachers and students move in and out. Yet, you will not want to move your children every year.

The **disadvantages of going to a school outside the neighborhood** may outweigh the advantages. Your children may find it difficult to separate from their neighborhood friends and endure longer rides to school and to the homes of friends. Providing daily transportation can be time-consuming and stressful for a family. Where there are several children attending different schools, this becomes even more complex.

It is often easier for children to attend extracurricular activities and after-school events at a school close to home. You, also, may find that involvement in your neighborhood school and local community will enable you to establish close ties with other families that will last for years.

Whether choosing to use the services of the public or private schools, or educate your children at home, you need to realize that **you are in the prime position to provide some essential teaching**. It is your interest in learning that will enable your children to become happy, productive human beings. From you they will learn to enjoy using their intelligence or fail to see the need to develop it.

What should I know about school curriculum?

Curriculum can vary from school to school, as well as from teacher to teacher. Some places have rigid requirements, and the teachers follow the standard curriculum. In other places teachers are more free to work closely with their students in deciding what to study. **Creative teachers,** however, **always seem to find interesting ways to teach any subject matter**.

Usually standardized tests used by districts dictate that certain material be mastered. There are basic reading, writing, and math concepts that most schools teach. How they are taught may vary greatly. By using this book's learning plan, **you are in the choicest place to make certain your children learn all they need to know**.

How can I recognize a good teacher?

Most educators seek to be good teachers. It is a demanding task—so demanding that many teachers leave the profession after only a few years in the classroom.

Certainly **good teachers love working with children. They are organized, good thinkers, and understand their subject matter and how to teach it. They model in themselves** those virtues of honesty, integrity, and respect, and set an example of the enthusiasm and creativity that they want to develop in their students.

Good teachers speak positively, and are able to create a pleasant and relaxed, yet businesslike, learning environment. Beyond that, there are many subtleties that are hard to identify. Often, you can only pinpoint excellence after your child has had a teacher for some time.

Talking with other parents can be helpful, but there are limitations. Some parents like teachers who have bubbly personalities and establish classrooms where kids have lots of fun. An educator who teaches children to work hard, to think broadly, and to be independent may not be as popular yet be a far better teacher for most children.

As you work with whatever teacher your child is assigned to, **keep in mind what teachers are expected to do**. Along with the fundamental knowledge and skills, they are to teach their students to enjoy learning and solving problems, know how to find, evaluate, and interpret information, learn to work with others, and develop good thinking skills.

Professional and legal duties require teachers to provide learning opportunities that teach respect for our differences. This includes treating our diverse cultures fairly, girls and boys equally, and providing for the learning styles and developmental needs of each student.

Classes usually have at least twenty-five students, and can include the physically, emotionally, and mentally challenged, those who have been abused, and those from dysfunctional homes. Along with covering the basic subjects, teachers are expected to develop in these students the values of respect for self as well as others, compassion, responsibility, honesty, integrity, and commitment to family and community.

Teachers must take time to meet with their assistants, other teachers, curriculum specialists, and parents as they plan their lessons. They serve on committees, attend professional meetings, read about educational developments, and train student teachers. All the while they must constantly be aware that they can be sued in court for any action or remark at which a parent feels offended.

To this agenda our society, in coping with its problems, continually adds new expectations for teachers. Additionally mandated programs may be valuable in themselves but can distract teachers from other important instruction. Time is so limited that educators must make hard choices on what and how much they can realistically do.

Teachers are to celebrate diversity with students, while knowing they may be expected to be less diverse and autonomous in their teamwork with colleagues. **School systems do not always reward the individuality and creativity of teachers.** Although they are expected to be fair and teach respect, their superiors may fail to show the same to them.

Most of all, today's teachers are supposed to be lively, creative thinkers! Yet school systems provide few incentives for this. Teachers are not always consulted in solving problems and making decisions that dramatically affect them. Rather, teachers who express their critical thinking aloud may actually be penalized because administrators believe it threatens them.

When evaluating educators, do not be surprised if a teacher seems uncertain in answering some questions. Much in education is changing and unstable today. An ambiguous situation can undermine a teacher's sense of security. Remember, we ask much of teachers while allowing support for them to be steadily eroded away.

Can I choose my children's teachers?

Some public schools allow parents to select teachers, and use a lottery system to equalize numbers when some teachers receive more requests than others. Such a system can recognize and encourage the good teachers.

Yet, while parents like it, some administrators do not. It is easier to manage a school by claiming that teachers are all comparatively equal. Less ambitious teachers like to think so, too.

Be alert to hidden agendas when a school is not interested in your teacher preferences. You know your child best. You know what kind of teacher will help you and your child to feel comfortable. Teachers are not all alike. Placement of students into classes can be very political!

Should I ask the administrators if I have questions about what is happening at school?

Always **try to solve school problems with the classroom teacher first.** Work closely with teachers because they are in the best position to help you. Taking everyday problems beyond the classroom can involve power struggles and politics.

Administrators hold their own influence over teachers and parents. Authoritarian ones control by making the decisions. Those with a laissez-faire attitude try to stay uninvolved and do not solve problems. Democratic leaders promote shared decision making which can create political conflict but also produces the most acceptable outcomes.

Administrators can exercise power with personnel evaluations and budgets. By politically passing out supplies and leadership roles they can align teachers against each other. When they threaten teachers with confidential parent information, it can affect the teachers' working relationship with students.

Remember that **you, too, can threaten teachers by what you say and do.** As a group, parents are often quite divided in their expectations of what schools can and should do. Some expect the impossible. The more vocal ones sometimes secure special favors for their children which may not be beneficial for the rest of the class. Others may blame schools for the frustrations they have with their children in their own home setting. It is important that you use tact and try to also see the teacher's point of view when discussing your children's school problems.

How should your children manage their school homework?

Nearly all teachers assign homework to extend the learning that takes place in the school day. You should welcome it, since this is usually the sign of a good teacher and a curriculum with high standards.

Whatever assignments they give, therefore, help your children see what they should learn from it and complete it in a reasonable amount of time. Ideally, the homework should be checked at school soon after it is completed, either by the students or the teacher. You may be able to make it more meaningful if you **connect it to their home learning plan.**

However, if your children are asked to do excessively long assignments or the work appears to be repetitive or meaningless, **discuss it with the teacher**. Share your concerns, information on your child's progress, and your willingness to help with the education.

Set realistic time plans for your family's homework. **Prioritizing activities helps them to be efficient time managers.** Encourage them to find ways to manage homework when the workload is especially heavy. Perhaps they can do more during school hours, rearrange time for home projects, or work together with friends.

Finally, there should be ample time in each day for your children to pursue activities of their own choosing. This can include club and church programs, music lessons, sports, and enjoyable reading.

How has technology affected schools?

New technologies add challenging new dimensions to learning. The use of videos can enrich some learning experiences but should not be overused. Many classrooms now have access to computers, CD ROMs, and the Internet to increase learning. Teachers, however, must not only know how to use these technologies but also how to select the best means to teach a given concept. Some classrooms have very limited learning technology, which may also be many years old. If the entire class does not have access to computers at the same time, their usefulness for whole class instruction is limited.

Furthermore, **technology is widening the gap** between students. Some children enrich their learning by being active home users of CD-ROMs and e-mail while others do not. School classes include both kinds of students and teachers must somehow narrow that gap.

As newer technologies provide for more specialized, effective, and rapid learning which can be done anywhere and at any time, our **expectations of schools will rise.** As a parent, you need to be aware of these technological potentials, and help your children gain the most from them.

How do schools handle discipline problems?

Every public school has problems with discipline today. Students now come to schools with more varying degrees of emotional pain and lack of family support. Some students are quite independent and self-assertive, less willing to follow directions and cooperate. They can disturb the school time for the eager learners. **Even excellent teachers can find it challenging** to teach a class with many disruptive students.

School staff members are quite limited in what they can do to prevent or punish disruptive behavior. Each school has a written discipline policy which you can obtain. Even with well written policies and specific consequences, however, it is difficult to deal with disruptive students. For many their inappropriate behavior is considered a disability and they have special rights. Furthermore, removal from regular classes can be considered unfair as it may be these students' only hope for success.

Are some school districts better than others?

Even a well-informed educator would find it difficult to compare one school district with another. It would take many lengthy observations to evaluate a given district, and most districts are very sensitive to critical visitors. Often teachers are not encouraged to visit other schools within their own district, let alone move about freely to enrich their teaching experiences.

It is also difficult to find reliable test information that compares one district with another. Educators readily admit that it is hard to construct good elementary skills tests, since so many variables can influence the results and children are continually growing and changing.

District test data comparisons, too, can leave educators unsettled and frantic in teaching to the test. As a result they naturally emphasize those things which can be objectively measured on tests.

We lack tests to accurately gauge progress in some of the most important concepts we teach, such as thinking skills, work habits, thought processes, attitudes and values.

The learning plan I present requires that **you evaluate progress through individual child-parent discussions**. It is difficult to do this kind of authentic testing within large groups. Whatever assumptions you draw about which districts are the best, you must constantly monitor your own children's progress and direct their programs to be assured of success.

CHAPTER 8

BE THEIR BEST TEACHER!

THIS book tells you what your children need to learn and describes why it is important that you take an active role in educating them. You know what they need to learn. **Now it is up to you to make sure that they learn all they need to know**. And even more, that they learn all they possibly can to best equip themselves for future success and happiness in a competitive technological world.

Through being closely involved in your children's education, **you can enrich your own life.** When you participate in their learning you will also learn and grow yourself. You will share in the pleasure that comes from helping children to learn and grow.

Today you can be assured that your children are making excellent academic progress by individualizing their learning yourself! You are in the best position to do this, and if you do not, for most children it will not happen. Then your youngsters will be left to learn random bits here and there, some parts overlapping and others missing altogether. They will be left without guidance to make sense out of what they do learn, sometimes confused and feeling insecure over the gaps in their knowledge. For example, your children will find themselves disadvantaged if they lack the breadth of skills needed in today's job market. Even their personal lives will be affected if they lack a broad knowledge base for developing their skills, making quality decisions, and relating to other people with many different values and cultures.

An added bonus will be that **your family living will benefit when you teach well.** The supportive environment needed to nurture good learning also helps families to be more caring and democratic and less hierarchical. It develops in everyone the character traits we all admire of being responsible and cooperative, having empathy and a good sense of humor.

You can pass your own values on to your children. They do not have to be left to learn mostly from television, peers, and other sources over which you have little control. You can protect your children from the economic, sexual, and material forces of today's world. With your close guidance they can experience childhood as an especially memorable time of innocence, appropriate learning, and fun.

So, commit yourself to it! You can do it. It is best for your children. Your children can grow up with your values which will return rewards to you. You can have fun in doing it. Your children can have every advantage that they need in order to succeed in today's global economy.

Seek to develop in yourself those qualities common to all good teachers. Be positive and enthusiastic. Be sensitive, caring and fair. Lead an exemplary lifestyle and share your enjoyment in continual learning. Be reasonable in your expectations. Support school teachers and learn from them; they have studied how best to teach specific concepts to groups of children. Also, even as you teach your children to be open to learning from different kinds of responsible people, teach them to be aware that what they hear and see may not always be objective, complete and honest.

You as parent can and must do what no one else can do for your children. **Be their best teacher!**